D1571899

G. KINGSLEY (KING) WARD, was born in Bathurst, New Brunswick, in 1932 and attended Mount Allison University and Queen's University. He joined Price Waterhouse Ltd. in 1955 and six years later embarked on his career as a highly successful independent businessman. Ward currently is president and owner of nine companies operating primarily in the field of health care. He is also the author of *Letters of a Businessman to his Son*, published in 1985.

G. KINGSLEY WARD

Letters of a Businessman to his Daughter

M&S

An M&S Paperback from
McClelland & Stewart Inc.
The Canadian Publishers

An M&S Paperback from McClelland & Stewart Inc.

First printing April 1990
Cloth edition printed 1989

Canadian Cataloguing in Publication Data

Ward, G. Kingsley.
Letters of a businessman to his daughter

(M&S paperback)
ISBN 0-7710-8803-5

1. Success.   2. Success in business.   3. Women in
business.   4. Conduct of life.   I. Title.

HF5386.W37 1990   650.1′02′4042   C89-095195-0

Cover design by Tad Aronowicz
Cover illustration by Robert Meecham

Printed and bound in Canada

McClelland & Stewart Inc.
The Canadian Publishers
481 University Avenue
Toronto, Ontario
M5G 2E9

To the most important women in my life: my mother, Elsie, my wife, Adele, and my daughter, Julie.

Contents

Preface

These letters were written from the heart with a great deal of love to my daughter, Julie.

Youth is a time which many older people look back on with envy; to carefree days untroubled by health problems, or family or job responsibilities, or financial setbacks. And many would agree with the writer who said, "Youth is such a wonderful thing; what a pity it is wasted on the young." Perhaps it is wasted, particularly when youth is experienced by the young as a time of insecurity, great unhappiness, and of defeat so great that, in many countries, suicide is the major cause of death in the fifteen to twenty-five year age group.

All too often, the burden of unhappiness is carried by youth alone and their desperation is unknown to their often very loving and caring parents. Communication breakdown between parents and children, of course, is chiefly responsible for the problem. Joseph Joubert said, "Ask the young: they know everything." And it is, of course, that attitude, which most of our young people adopt at some stage or another, that particularly sets us parents off, and which sends both sides veering in opposite directions. We tend to forget that it is no more than the flexing of young wings we hear, preparatory to fleeing the family nest – just as we did in our bid for freedom and independence and the right to test adulthood in our own wide open spaces. Maintaining a strong communication with our children can be extremely difficult during this phase, and if lack of respect for their needs enters the picture, the gulf between the two sides can sometimes take years to bridge again.

I wholeheartedly endorse the theory that achievement is the core of happiness; not necessarily achievement above others', but achievement for oneself–in whatever subject, at whatever plane. Achievement requires effort; effort requires encouragement. The young, who are particularly vulnerable both to making mistakes and to overreacting to their disappointments, most especially require encouragement–and the best kind is strong parental enthusiasm and support. That is what I most desire to offer my daughter.

In these letters to her I have expressed some of my personal views on life and on business. There are no attempts to sermonize, or to lecture, or to issue edicts. There is no treatise on business theory. Throughout, instead, I present what I believe are the fundamental, tried-and-true, common-sense tenets of both topics, and reminders to review these tenets often for they tend to be neglected as we try to keep pace with life in the fast lane.

I have written these letters in the hope that a quiet written word on a subject will be regarded more as an observation gleaned from experience than as a rigid command or pronouncement. Someone once asked me if my son was heeding my advice published in *Letters of a Businessman to his Son*. I replied that I hoped so. What I know for certain is that it has saved us several heated arguments. On such occasions, I would simply suggest he read chapter so-and-so from that book before we got too steamed up and, generally, agreeable communication followed. The written word has an impact and a staying power which often far surpasses the effect of talking, especially if the conversation is either so emotionally charged or so loud that it only turns off the mind and ears of the listener.

Around the world, more and more women are choosing careers outside the home; many are breaking new ground and gaining unprecedented achievements for their sex. It has taken women years of courage and perseverance to accomplish this, and their breakthrough will be to the benefit of us all. New lifestyles for couples have emerged, which should strengthen our marriages and improve the quality of care given our children in their early years: an improvement stemming from the sharing of parenting by both parents.

Certainly, there are challenges unique to a two-career family that must be addressed and overcome; certainly, communication lines must be kept wide open. Both partners must be flexible and willing to make compromises, and both must be supportive of the other's careers and values. It *can* work; women already know that. All that is left is for many men to alter their attitudes about career relocations, about changing diapers and taking the kids to the pediatrician, or about washing dishes and doing the weekly grocery shopping.

It is interesting to me that many of the maxims left to us in the writings of such great people as Confucius, Lao Tzu, Aristotle, Horace, Shakespeare, Bacon, Goethe, Emerson, Thoreau, and countless others, are no different than those told to me by my mother and father (and probably by yours) in their later years. Mine had not read any of the above men's writings, yet they had learned many of the same lessons. And in all likelihood, they would all concur with Sören Kierkegaard's observation that, "Life can only be understood backwards; but it must be lived forwards."

Given encouragement, given perspectives and insights that help them to understand how the pieces of life fit together, there is nothing our youth cannot accomplish or achieve. Toward that end these letters were written – primarily to my daughter, but also, with love, to all young people brave enough to reach for a dream, fail, try again, and again, and ever again, until they succeed.

Acknowledgements

In 1985, my son and I argued strenuously against the publication of my private letters to him. His mother – my wife – Adele, argued just as strongly that others could benefit from reading these letters, and in the end we reluctantly agreed to publish them, with the caveat, "Nobody will buy the book." So much for male opinion. That book, *Letters of a Businessman to his Son*, has been published in eight languages, in twelve countries, and has sold over one million copies.

After that success, I was ready to retire as an amateur author, but was persuaded by my wife, and others, to complement my first book with a second, addressed to my daughter. This second book, as was the first, was edited by Adele, who laboured to correct my misuse of the English language far into the night, after full days spent running her own company.

The manuscript, however, still required a professional to put it into suitable form for a book. That task fell to my editor, Dinah Forbes, who, with care and respect, moulded the messages that I wrote for my daughter and for other young women and men starting out in a career in business.

So, to Dinah and Adele, my heartfelt thanks.

1 New Beginnings

Dear Quivering Knees:

I know you are on pins and needles, and facing tomorrow with dread. You are starting a new school—high school, at that—and there will not be even one friend there you can count on for some moral support. A change is about to occur in your young life, and you are not looking forward to it one bit. But as sure as the sun rises and sets each day, so will changes continue to ebb and flow through your life. Why approach them with fear when you have the choice of facing them with optimism? Let us examine your worries about tomorrow and, perhaps, between the two of us, we can allay some of your apprehension.

You will not know a soul at this new school, and you are panicky about having to strike up new friendships. Fair enough. Initially, you will have to walk the strange halls feeling all alone, although surrounded by a lot of people, and that can be a little frightening. But your loneliness needn't last for long.

There will be other newcomers in that crowd feeling just as jittery and shy as you; others needing a new friend just as badly as you. How about trying to seek them out? I guarantee that by the simple act of just looking to help someone else in his or her loneliness, you will soon forget about your own. It's as good as magic. And somewhere in that crowd *is* one (or several) of life's most precious treasures: a good and true friend.

I believe that we should be quite selective in our choice of friends. Knowing you, I think you will want to befriend someone who is kind, who likes to laugh and does so easily, and someone whom you feel you can trust. You will find your kind of person, but bear in mind that the easiest way of winning a new friend is to first *be* a friend. Do not misconstrue this as meaning that you should overwhelm that person with elaborate acts of great kindness and thoughtfulness at first or second meeting. There is a blending-in period, which must flower on its own as two people get to know one another better. Demonstrate your fine characteristics on a consistent basis, and you will find your friendship growing a little stronger and deeper each new day.

Sometimes, as you get to know him or her better, the person you thought would be a good friend turns out to be not so pleasant; a dud. It is disappointing, of course, but don't unduly agonize over a lost cause; concentrate on finding a worthy replacement instead. It is my impression and it has been my experience that the best friends to have are those who not only are always there to lend a sympathetic ear when you are down, but those who, just as readily, are always there when you are up, to share your joys and happinesses with you. I know I don't have to remind you to always ''be there''–both ways–for your friends.

Some friendships last forever. Unfortunately, many do not. But when a friendship ends–as in all likelihood some of yours will–do not start berating yourself for its demise as if it were all your fault. Although it does take two to start an argument and only one to end it, no friendship thrives if it is always the same person who ends the disputes. It takes "two to tango" in step with one another most of the time. Moreover, there is a fine balance of chemistry involved in a relationship between two people, and sometimes it vanishes for no apparent reason. However, even when a closeness dissolves, I feel that any past good friendship deserves some continuation of loyalty in times of need or emergency on either side. Extending that familiar helpful hand to a former good friend is a uniquely rewarding experience.

Someone once said, "You can tell a lot about a person by the company he keeps." Pick good friends, because I know you deserve the best – even if I am a little biased about your many fine qualities.

Now let us turn our attention to your academic concerns. You are used to getting high marks and are proud of it – but since the work will be more challenging now, you are worried about being able to maintain your excellent grades. You needn't worry; it is no cause for alarm. If you increase your study time and your effort accordingly, those good marks you want will be just as forthcoming as ever. And when you analyse the poor marks you receive (only a few, I hope), and you are truthful, I think you will realize that you just had not given that particular subject the amount of study it had demanded. Some courses will require much more work than others. Separate those that are the hardest for you and give them your first priority, then allocate study time to the rest of your curriculum in like manner.

The human mind has the capacity of absorbing a great deal of information in one day, but I believe that there is a limit to what it can effectually assimilate. Feeding it a steady flow of information daily builds a mountain of knowledge by the end of the year. Beware, however, of trying to jam all the data you need on a subject into your mind during just the week or two before exams. Some people get away with this tactic for a while, but sooner or later, most fall by the wayside when time runs out and work loads increase.

Habit is a two-adjective word: good and bad. One of the prerequisites of success is a good studying habit developed early in life. A poor, lackadaisical pattern of studying or a casual attitude towards learning during early years becomes all the more difficult to reverse the more time goes on and can cause some agonizing defeats and disappointments in later years. *Please* cement your good study habits now, so I can enjoy your exam results with you – and so you can prevent my agony (double please) upon seeing you in tears over your marks.

A few more words of advice, if I may. Your school encourages participation in a number of activities outside the classroom. Take a good look at what is being offered in sports, music, art, photography, and other fields, and get involved. The mind gets bored with a constant barrage of work, so put your study habits in place and then pursue your other interests. You will find that both your mind and your body will benefit from the change. When your body feels better, as it usually does after sports or recreation, so does your mind; it is rested, refreshed, and more receptive when you return to your studies. A nice combination of "pluses"; a nice balance in life.

Over the next few months you will form some new, warm, and, I hope, long-lasting friendships. Your mother and I look forward to meeting your new friends and to their visiting our home often. Of course, we also dearly hope that you will enjoy your new school and be delighted with your achievements inside and outside the classroom. Please be sure to understand, however, that we set no levels of accomplishment for you to attain. Those levels must be set by *you*, for they are your goals in life – not ours, as much as we are interested in them. Our review of your report card will not be of the marks the teacher gives you, but of the mark you give yourself for effort. Some 50 per cent marks require double the work of some 80 per cent marks. Keep your effort at 100 per cent; the marks will follow.

And do not be afraid of Spenser's "ever-whirling wheel of Change." In my view, change is but another of nature's laws to provoke initiative.

With much love,

Daddy

2 Career Choosing

My Dear Daughter:

Your high school years will soon come to an end, and I have noticed that choosing a career for yourself has become a matter of great concern and growing uncertainty for you. You are not alone, dear. Most young people facing this same weighty decision feel just as insecure about making it as you do. It is a period of indecisiveness, which has plagued the young since time immemorial. Some older people chalk all this uncertainty up to "the vagary of youth." I do not. I think it is we – the older generation – who are to blame for your fogginess and bewilderment at this crossroads in your life.

As adults, we have failed miserably at providing your age group with enough sound and practical information upon which you can secure your judgements about future careers. How can you decide to be an engineer without an inkling of the dozens of different facets grouped under the title "engineering"? Have you any idea what the work of a doctor or of a lawyer or of a geologist really entails? Of course not; you've never seen their work from their perspective. The best thing would be for someone to take the time and effort to guide you through the daily routines of the professions in which you are interested. In my opinion, there is no better method of gaining effectual knowledge about them.

I am happy to say that I helped implement a program along these lines at your brother's school. There, for a period of a week, we assembled a group of speakers from about twelve different professions. The students first listened to overviews of each of the twelve speakers' areas of expertise and then each young person selected at least two careers of particular interest to him. We then made arrangements for the students to visit the work places of the professions they had chosen: a hospital for the aspiring doctors, a computer programming company for those interested in that field, and so on.

Following these visits, many of the young people in our course changed their minds about the careers they had thought would interest them, while others became even more enthusiastic about pursuing the fields of their choice. Best of all, of course, was that they had all sampled a little taste of some of the different ways they could go about earning a living.

Now a week is certainly not enough time to devote to a project of this importance with the hopes of producing concrete results. But at least this school is doing *something* along more practical lines than simple verbal counselling to help their students select jobs that they will be happy doing twenty years down the pike.

In the past, most career opportunities were open only to men. Your grandmother's career potential was set for her the day she was brought into this world: bearing children and tending house. Down through all the ages, only a handful of positions, such as teaching and nursing, were considered suitable employment for women. It was a "man's world" out there in the work place; "a woman's place was in the home." (Where the *real* work was, I have often thought. I doubt it was a man in those days who coined the saying, "A man works from sun to sun while a woman's work is never done.")

In this very rapidly changing world of ours, the role of child bearer is still exclusively the woman's (for which fact most men would probably thank God), but now a huge number of women are working outside the home. When I studied for my chartered accountants degree, it was rare to see a woman in the course (much to my wandering eyes' sorrow, for I was single at the time). Today, thirty years later, about 35 per cent of graduates are of your sex, and the same trend applies in most other fields: law, policing, business management, engineering, architecture, medicine, and so on. Now, practically any field of work is open to you for consideration. But with so many avenues to explore, how do you go about narrowing them down? It can be done.

Ten years is a long time in your life's calendar at the moment, but try to project yourself ahead ten years in time. What work do you most picture yourself doing then, happily and contentedly? Thinking in these long-range terms, make a list of the careers that appeal to you most, and then bring a number of other factors into play. How good are you at the courses you need to enter that particular field? What is the lifestyle of that career? For instance, policewomen have to work shifts; would you mind that? Are employment opportunities limited, as are those faced, for example, by a marine biologist or an archaeologist? What are the geographic areas of work? A geologist has to spend a lot of time away from home searching for new mineral resources; how would such a requisite fit in with your family life? Unless you feel a very strong pull toward a certain field of work, I would recommend you choose one that affords work opportunities in almost any location, so that all you would have to do is take your talents with you, should you decide to move from one place to another. Many doctors find moving from one country to another extremely difficult because of the stringent requirements pertaining to their education, which vary almost country by country. Even moving within a country can be

21

tough if state or provincial laws governing your profession are not uniform.

How to blend child-raising with a career is another issue for deliberation by both men and women before they choose a career. Some couples have circumvented the entire matter by deciding not to have children. I am sure it is possible to have a greatly fulfilling and happy life without children, but having enjoyed my life so enormously as a parent of you and your brother, I am convinced that children bring a certain quality of joy surpassed by none other. (Especially if the children are like you!)

If you plan to have children, give special consideration to how they are going to be looked after in their early years. Numerous psychologists say that adult stability – or the lack thereof–is mainly determined during the first three years of life: whether the adult as a child during those first crucial years felt loved or unloved, calm and content, or nervous and insecure. Many couples have no choice but for both to work outside the home, but if you have a choice, you might want to be the one to choose a career that can be interrupted while you raise your children for a few years and then resumed without too much difficulty or setback when they are of school age. Then, again, you might prefer a career that can be continued on a consulting or freelance basis from home during early child-raising years. (As you know, your mother switched from a senior advertising executive's position to freelance writing at home while raising your brother and you and became one of our country's top writers of children's television programs.) But it is all a highly personal matter and one that should be carefully considered and decided upon only by the two parents involved.

Looking into the future can be murky, but as Lao Tzu pointed out, ''A journey of a thousand miles must begin with a single step.'' So start daydreaming now of what you think you would like to be doing ten years from now. Together, if you will allow me the privilege of helping, we will whittle your dreams down to two or three career pursuits, discuss them thoroughly, and then set up our own visits to the work places of each. From among our many friends, I am sure we will be able to locate several engaged in the fields of your choice who would be delighted to be of help to any extent. (We older folk truly enjoy helping young people in matters of such importance, probably because we've made so many mistakes of our own along the way that we would love to see you and your young friends avoid making the same.) I am optimistic that, at the end of our program, you will be able to arrive at some sound conclusions about your future with a good amount of confidence – and a huge amount of renewed high spirits.

I would like to leave you with one more thought before closing. This *is* a serious decision-making period of your life, but do not overlook that it is also one of the most exciting and wondrous of all times: the threshold of doing anything you want to do, becoming anything you want to be. Pause. Give it a moment's reflection. Then let your spirits soar.

With much love,

Your Guidance Counsellor

3 On Failure

My Dear Gloomy Gus:

For the past few days, I must admit, you have not been the easiest person to live with. It has become rather irksome hearing you call yourself a dummy, a total failure, and moaning that your life has been smashed to smithereens as if it were a piece of china. A shattered piece of china can never be put back together again; its useful life is over. Your useful life has only just begun.

Yes, being refused entrance to the university of your dreams is a tough blow, and a mighty big pill for you to have to swallow. It is your first major disappointment. But you had better toughen up and get used to those, for along with all the goodies, letdowns, too, are a part of life. Much more important, though, you should understand clearly that disappointments will do you in if you continue viewing each as you are this one: a collosal failure instead of a temporary setback and a *challenge* to be conquered. Disappointments become failures only if you *allow* them to become so by failing to try again.

In *All's Well That Ends Well*, the Bard wrote, "Oft expectation fails, and most oft there where most it promises." Your many successful school years had led you to believe that acceptance in your first choice of colleges would be automatic. It had probably existed as a foregone conclusion for you for a long time. There is a lesson to be learned here: Take nothing for granted when important steps in your life need to be climbed. Always, always, have a backup plan in readiness should a first, second, or even third stair collapse at your approach. No alternatives in place to fall back on makes this disappointment all the more painful and difficult for you to accept. I was remiss in not having discussed with you the importance of such pre-planning in the event that what happened might happen, for which I apologize.

But let us both pick up your socks now and move on. Life is full of twists, and as you grow older, more and more will present themselves. That is a simple fact of life. But it will be up to you what you actually label those curves and, subsequently, how you handle them. You can accept my suggestion and take them on as the challenges I mentioned earlier, or you can go along with a lot of other people who tag them problems, or misfortunes, or crises, or rotten breaks, or any other feeble excuse for feeling beaten before ever once having tried a better outlook. A fellow by the name of Frank Ward O'Malley said, "Life is just one damned thing after another." He was a beaten man when he said that.

Review your present state of affairs: You have finished high school with good marks, you have shown courage and determination both inside and outside of school, your health is excellent, your looks are quite lovely, your home is comfortable and secure, your parents' love is constant, you hold down a fine part-time job, and your boyfriend likes you. That's quite a lot of great things to have going for you. But now there's a bit of a "downer" in the piece. What to do about it?

Well, to start, when I last counted, there was more than one good university in this country offering the courses you wish to pursue. How about shedding the "I am a failure" attitude in favour of "I am an optimist," and immediately making enquiries at these other schools? Your high school record is very good, and I am certain that a concerted try at applying to other universities will pay off.

You wish to study business management. The text books used in the university of your first choice are exactly the same as those used in the classrooms of others. The professors are different, of course, but it is *you*, not one of the profs you will encounter, who has first claim on your future. So, *on* with your claim on life. It really isn't over yet, as much as you have been trying to convince me of late that it is. You will find that there are many events in a lifetime that, devastating as they might appear to be when they occur, are the very catalysts that set us on new and better directions.

Many young people give up their quest for a chosen career because of exactly the same barrier facing you now. They back off, claim fate is being mean to them, and they become intimidated by what they believe is a loss of control. It is a sad response, for it is not occurrences that shape our lives but how we *use* those occurrences to shape our lives. It is not the world against you; it is you challenging the world during tough times, and you refusing to be beaten. Giving up is easier, of course; lots of people prove that every day of their existence. But those are not the people walking around, tall as the trees, their heads held high, as I think you wish to be. When one door slams shut in your face, go and knock on the next door, and bang on the next, and the next, until one opens up with acceptance. Those who learn to do this early in life cannot help but gain extraordinary success.

We cannot all be kings or queens, but that is about all most of us truly cannot ever be. Most other aspirations are within reach if you condition your mind to respond ever positively to those twists of life. Tell yourself over and over again, "I *am* going to win, *I* am going to win, I am going to *win*," and in time you will find your mind almost automatically advising you what to do next, for its primary function is to weigh all your facts and unravel any solutions you might need.

Ask any successful person how he or she "got there," and you will hear of persistence, of challenges, and of the detours that often had to be taken before the desired goal was reached. Your university rejection – any rejection – can be detoured with startlingly fine results – if you but evict failure from your mind and never allow it to roost there or in your heart again.

Start looking for those detours. They are unmarked but, believe me, they are there, near every rock or stump on which you might stub a toe.

Love,

Your Detour Guide

4 Self-Respect

My Disillusioned Daughter:

What a letdown it was, hearing that the big party you had so looked forward to last Saturday was a disaster and a source of great embarrassment for several of your young friends, most especially for one of your closest friends. Having a good time is one thing, having a good time that demeans oneself and offends others is quite a different matter. Obviously, your friend's joviality lapsed into the second category.

I take it she got totally carried away and performed some pretty unusual antics of which she is now highly ashamed. As you say, perhaps she had just tried too hard to be the hit of the party and it boomeranged on her at a terrible cost: the loss of her all-round respect. But a moment's stupidity often backfires that way, causing us days, weeks, or even months of feeling shame and self-reproach.

Needless to say, I am extremely happy and proud (and thankful!) that you survived this party with no distortion of your fine image. I hope you will always continue to hold firm your own self-respect and the respect of all who know you, for it is probably the most valuable jewel of life.

Having people respect you means that you are being held in high regard for your moral values. It goes without saying that it is difficult to respect a thief, a prostitute, an alcoholic, a drug user, or anyone who abuses or corrupts either themselves or others in the pursuit of money, power, or so-called fun. But such extremes aside, it seems to me that maintaining one's self-respect and that of others while going through youthful years is a particularly hazardous affair.

It is only human to want to have friends and to feel accepted and liked by other people – a desire that is more pronounced in youth than in later years. Particularly among the young there is all too often one unfortunate person who is refused acceptance by "the crowd" because of a lack of personality (which has probably not yet even fully developed), or a lack of attractiveness, or a lack of some kind of sports or arts ability. In short, such a person appears to own none of the attributes that normally attract one person to another or that cause other people to want to be in his company. This can be dangerous for the outcast for, in his overzealous pursuit of friendship and in his desire to become "one of the gang," he often starts behaving as he thinks others want him to behave and not at all according to his own finer instincts. He drinks to excess, and/or gets hooked on drugs, and/or steals (if not for money, for the "adventure"), and/or abuses people, sometimes sexually, to prove either his cool worldliness or his physical strength. Inevitably, one morning, he wakes up wondering where his self-esteem went and when it left.

I do not believe that youthful years are any more perilous now than they have ever been, but there is no doubt that they are and always have been the most treacherously challenging of all. Fortunately, many of the hazards of these years almost magically start disintegrating as maturity and the assumption of adult responsibilities begin. Until this natural transition occurs, however, it would be prudent to heed the admonition of Marcus Aurelius Antonius of about 160 A.D.: "Never esteem anything as of advantage to you that shall make you break your word or lose your self-respect."

Unnerved by your friend's shocking behaviour, you stated that you never want to find yourself in a similar position and asked how you can make sure that you never do. Well, for one thing, it takes some thinking *beforehand*. For a start, travel with a group of friends who, like you, wish to avoid any activities that might bring disrepect to themselves or to their families. If that is hard to accomplish, then finding even one good friend who is of strong moral fibre is a great help. It is a big world out there and facing it all by yourself on some occasions can be a lonely battle. You will learn to confront it alone in time, but during these growing years, you can do with a little moral support now and then. As one voice in a crowd, you can feel as ineffectual as a mouse but, although one friend and you equals only two, that second person's support is often worth the strength of an army. The same, of course, applies the other way – when your friend might need backup for his or her point of view.

Another good, precautionary method of avoiding disgraceful behaviour is to imagine the personal hurt it would inflict upon your family. Aside from bringing dismay or embarrassment or even financial expenses down on their heads to bail you out of some legal predicament, think of the agony involved – theirs and yours – in their losing respect for you. There are consequences to every action; some thought given to them beforehand is a great protector of self-esteem.

Because your self-respect and conscience would suffer if you did not, try to help your friend now that she is in trouble. Now is the time to go to her and prove to her that you are a true friend in tough times as well as in good. It builds character to help another in times of trouble – especially in such as this, which presents the opportunity of trying to shield her from repeating her mistake on future occasions. A word of caution, though: gauge your friend's progress and decide whether she is sincerely trying to clean up her act. Some people learn nothing from their mistakes, and any effort to help them is as futile as trying to stop Niagara Falls from falling. By your friend's future behaviour, you will have to judge whether she is or is not deserving of your continued friendship and allegiance. Some people are not. And I reemphasize that your best method of warding off unnecessary trouble is by being discerning in your selection of friends.

I should like to think that I have taught you well about handling alcohol with care; that if it is used, it should be only for relaxation or fun and never in courting disaster. And you know my feelings about drugs—that if there must be a choice between drugs or alcohol, you would be much better off to stick to alcohol. It has one main ingredient, ethyl alcohol, and your body is geared to throw off its effects, even those of over-consumption, within twenty-four hours. Human beings have had a lot of experience with alcohol and its effects on the body, so we know what we are dealing with here. Not so with drugs. The use of drugs is still a fairly recent development within our society and the effects of the many chemical combinations in drugs, both hard and soft, on the human system have yet to be determined. Marijuana alone contains over four hundred separate chemical properties, some of which remain in the body for a long time. The long-term effects of many such drugs, because of their multi-facet make-up, is still a profoundly disconcerting unknown. An alcoholic's chances of resuming normal bodily health once he stops imbibing liquor are usually quite good. That is a known. But only time can yet prove what a drug abuser's long-term health prospects are once he kicks his lethal habit. Scary, scary business!

And don't for a moment believe as some do, that the avoidance of a hangover is some special advantage of taking certain drugs over alcohol. It is a foolish and dangerous delusion. A hangover is your body's built-in policing system telling you that you had too much to drink the night before. Of what advantage are no warning signals that you smoked or snorted or shot up too much the night before?

Enjoy your parties but, I repeat, if you must choose between booze or drugs, stick to booze. Not only is it the less potential hazard to your health of the two, it is legal to consume. (But if you do drink at parties, be sure to give me a call for a lift home.)

The sex scene is another area fraught with potential dangers. When the Good Lord made us, He included sexual drive among all the other many good things with which He endowed us. At times, however, I am sure that many feel He almost over-charged our bodies with sexual desire – why else is it so hard on some occasions to curb our emotions so that they do not override our moral standards? Hard it is at times, but I can assure you that the extra effort on those occasions is worth the mighty reward of feeling proud of the strength of your convic-tions. Again, the consequences of all our actions and how we feel about ourselves – good or bad in their wake – is, I believe, what matters most in this department, just as it does in all other areas of our lives. Self-respect cannot exclude respect for our bodies.

This letter could go on forever on the topic of self-respect and the sundry ways it can be squandered, shattered, or battered. Far more important, is that its value be esteemed and regarded as vital to our well-being as is the air we breathe. Living without it is hardly living at all.

Robert Louis Stevenson said, "Youth is wholly experimen-tal." Please pick your experiments carefully and perspica-ciously. (And yes, you might have to look up that last word in your dictionary.)

Love,

Daddy

5 Mind before Matter

Dear Winner:

Congratulations! You've made it, and I could not be a prouder father. I greatly share in your joy of having achieved the goal you have spent most of your life so far pursuing. School is out: No more exams! You have completed your formal education and your new life is beginning. Now all you can think of is getting out in the real world, landing a great job, living on your own, buying a car, and so on and so forth. But it is at this most wonderful moment of your life thus far that I must ask you to reign in all such thoughts and back up a step or two with me. There will never be a topic of greater importance than the one I wish to present to you now.

All your objectives are valid and wildly exciting and positive, and I dearly hope that every single one of them comes off just as you wish, without a hitch. But herein lies my question: If one or more do not, how well prepared are you to handle the accompanying disappointments? How well equipped are you to handle *any* challenge that may appear on your horizon?

In other words, what is your master plan, your guiding principle? You *must* have one if you are to achieve the dizzying heights of success and happiness to which you aspire and if you are to put to fullest use all these hard years of schooling.

How do you do it? By first and foremost—and always—studying the workings of the mind. That's right, by studying the workings of the mind, for it is the polestar of all of our actions. How well you understand the mind's method of operation, the ways it can make you or break you, is a very major piece of knowledge; a giant step toward achieving success.

How many people do you know who are always "up," always "with it," always bright on a bleak day? Notice how quickly they come to mind? It is not surprising, for they are outstanding. (Unfortunately, they are probably not as many as we would all like to include among our friends and acquaintances, and especially among our relatives!) But have you ever wondered why one person is always cheerful and another almost always downcast? It is my firm belief that neither was just born that way, but that one practises being up by mentally refusing to be down, while the other does not even know she could try. What a waste of time, feeling depressed, when we could just as readily feel great. All it takes is a little understanding of the mind and how it works.

The mind operates on two levels: the conscious and the subconscious. No better analogy of the subconscious mind could be given than that it performs as your own, personally programmed computer. The conscious section has the responsibility of governing your thoughts and choices, while the subconscious runs your body actions and senses, and acts as your memory bank and your creative engine. Few people realize that what you enter into your subconscious is exactly what you will eventually get back in the way of personality traits, character, and even well-being. In other words, you are your own computer programmer and the mistress of your destiny.

With your conscious mind, you can choose which thoughts you want stored in your subconscious memory bank and which you do not. You alone are responsible for the contents of this memory bank – and it is its inventory that shapes your character and determines your outlook, your health, and your prospects. Shovel in a lot of garbage, such as fear, worry, envy, doubt, and anxiety, on a consistent basis, and you will get back the same in return: pure garbage fuelling your creative engine and moulding and controlling your life. Fuel it, instead, with steadfast thoughts of strength, hope, confidence, perseverence, love, forgiveness, courage, and you will experience yourself moving from one achievement to another, even those beyond your hopes, expectations, and aspirations. As James Allen said, "You think in secret, and it comes to pass; your environment is but your looking glass."

If it's so simple, you ask, why isn't all this common knowledge? Because it is not taught in our schools; our media does not feature it in broadcasts or on the front pages of our newspapers; and because most of us do not read to learn after we leave school. It is a costly omission, for from within the subconscious mind came the imagination to invent the light bulb, the telephone, the polio vaccine, the space shuttle, and the world's finest literature and art. What such wonderful – or better – accomplishments might now lie dormant under the weight of negative input in your subconscious? Think about it. Are they never to surface? They can – easily – by training your conscious mind always to say No to all thoughts of insecurity, fear, depression, guilt, anxiety, or worry; by refusing them entry into that precious storehouse of your subconscious mind. Although you may not be able to erase the negative thoughts already stowed there, you can certainly crowd their space and render them powerless against a steady stream of positive input, and in time, with enough positive programming, you will find your conscious mind automatically rejecting negative thoughts. Then you will really start living, achieving, and relishing life as it is meant to be. You will move in a spirit of confidence – sure-footed, and undaunted by whatever might come your way. The results are marvellous.

Constant repetition of your positive thoughts and ideas is vitally important; it is a key factor during this process. It will require *time, concentration* and *persistence* on your part, but once the mind is programmed in the right direction, you will find it is virtually addicted to success and impervious to defeat. You will also have learned the value of *now*. No longer will any memory haunt you or any past mistake encumber you. You will have learned how to select only the best from yesterday to put to work for you today. Nor will tomorrow worry you because you will have learned that worry is destructive, that it never yet has solved a problem, so why allow it valuable space in your mind?

Emotions should be expressed. They are part of our mental makeup, and stress levels can run pretty high if our feelings are not articulated or aired. But train the mind to separate the wheat from the chaff in this department, too. For instance, expressing anger to get it out and over with when it occurs is healthy; suppressing it until it becomes a festering boil of resentment is unhealthy and a major hindrance to character growth. Fear in life-threatening circumstances is normal; most other fears should be viewed as abnormal. They are caused by ignorance, and they can virtually paralyse your moving ahead.

Assess your emotions carefully, especially those primarily fuelled by anger, jealousy, revenge, or fear. These are strong and very destructive feelings, which will impede your progress more severely than any other I know. On the other hand, nurture such feelings as those of love, friendship, compassion, benevolence, and humour. Not only do they produce immediately rewarding results of satisfaction and a good feeling about yourself, but they tend to possess a boomerang quality, a return "in kind" – usually many times over.

Once your positive input is consistent, start paying serious attention to intuition. This is an innate knowledge from somewhere deep within, which sometimes insists that "this is right" or that "that is wrong" when there is little or no tangible proof to support it. On many an occasion I have studied a problem long and hard, and from inside out and upside down, to arrive at a logical conclusion, only to alter it because of that sixth sense or that quiet internal voice which insisted I do so. Seldom has it steered me wrong. It is a wisdom surfacing from your subconscious, obtained partly by reason, partly by perception, to tell you there *is* another solution even though it cannot be clearly defined at the time. The wise person has learned to heed his intuition. As a matter of fact, many successful people *rely* on hunches or gut feelings during times of difficult decision-making and feel totally comfortable about it although they cannot rationally explain why. These confident people know that intuition often decides what researched facts, reason, and conscious thinking sometimes cannot decide.

Relying on intuition, however, does not preclude the necessity of attaining an education, nor the hard work of compiling all available facts and figures pertaining to a given problem, nor the application of reason and sound logical thinking to its solution. But once you've done all this and a solution still remains elusive or murky, submit the problem to what Thoreau called "the treasury of the mind"–your subconscious–and then relax and quietly listen to your inner voice. The answer may take time, but do not force it. You will know it when it comes. It is exciting to experience a feeling so strong that you are drawn, irresistibly, in a particular direction without wholly understanding why. Learn to develop trust in your intuition. You will discover that a great many more times than not, it is leading you in the right direction.

What has all this "mind stuff" to do with your finding a job and new living quarters, and borrowing money for a car? Believe me, it is the first crucial step toward all your life's objectives. Heed it, and the rest will be easy. Joseph Conrad put it this way: "The mind of man is capable of anything – because everything is in it, all the past as well as all the future."

I have stated several times that the technique of forming your mind to react positively is easy. Here's why: Most of us use only a minute portion of the tremendous reservoir of latent talents we all possess. Needless to say, that leaves a lot of room for expansion because the potential of the mind has not yet even begun to be tapped. We will discuss your desired goals at another time, but before any are set, get your mind computer in good running order first by diligently practising positive thinking.

One word of warning: Few have attained success without their methods of getting there being challenged, attacked, ridiculed, or criticized by others. Such judgements matter, but only because of their corrosive power which, of course, must be countered with stronger and more persistent positive energy. If talking about "mind stuff" such as written here turns any of your friends or associates off, change the subject to one of less import – for where you're going, they will probably never reach, and I doubt you will note their absence when you get there. Persons with tight little minds tend to be most "forgettable."

Please study this letter carefully. It contains the most valuable advice with respect to your future that I could ever possibly try to give you.

Love,

Sigmund

6 The Importance
of Setting Goals

Dear Daughter:

I like the way your eyes light up whenever your cousin, Johnny, is around. You are very proud of him, and with just cause. His achievements during the first thirty years of his life are many and mighty. He has set his winning course and learned well how to keep to it. It is heartening to see this fine young man doing so superbly, and I, too, am very proud of him.

Your words the other day, ''How come there are so few successful people around like my cousin?'', started me thinking. But before we get into that, let me ask if you are aware of the tinge of wistfulness in your voice every time you speak of Johnny? If it is because you are mentally comparing your achievements to his each time and feel disheartened by the results, it is a dangerous practice and one which must be curtailed. On the other hand, analysing an achiever's winning methods to put them to good use for yourself is a valuable exercise. Do the latter, and forget the former. If your hint of yearning stems from a bit of envy, that is only human. But even then, make sure that it stays a bit, and never becomes a lot. Envy is the sustenance of non-doers – a group to which you do not belong.

Now let's see if we can figure out "what makes Johnny tick?" with the intent of putting a lot of what we learn to work for you.

First, of course, there is his unswerving belief in himself and in what he can accomplish. He seems always to "expect the best"; always to exude optimism, hope, and desire. Seldom have I seen that young man downcast, and never so for long. He has learned that a positive attitude is one of our greatest strengths and he has trained his mind to behave accordingly. But all of this you have already learned. Now for more.

William James had this to say about most of us: "Most people live, whether physically, intellectually, or morally, in a very restricted circle of their potential being. They make use of a very small portion of their possible consciousness and of their soul's resources in general, much like a man who, out of his whole bodily organism, should get into a habit of using and moving only his little finger."

Johnny sure as hell has learned how to use a great deal more than a little finger's worth of his potential in all three of Mr James's zones. This is another "secret" of his success, which is as available to all of us as the air we breathe. How does he do it? By setting *goals* for himself and carefully laying out methods of achieving them – the very thing most of us fail to do and, as a result, spend our lives as one lost in the woods without a compass, walking about in circles, and getting nowhere.

You have said that many of your friends don't know what they want out of life. Obviously, that is the very first major decision to make. *Define your goals.* There are both personal goals and career goals to think about. What do you want most to achieve in each of them? Or, put it more succinctly, what do you want most from life? Enumerate your targets and then measure your depth of desire for each carefully, for desire is the energy that fuels the moral stamina you will need to attain them. This is your first important move if you are to step out of that "restricted circle of our potential being" about which Mr James speaks.

Your next is to map out a course of action. An eminent present-day speaker, Bob Proctor, tells his audiences, "You can achieve anything if, upon selecting your goals, you *plan* how to reach them, for they will not just drop in your lap." You must figure out your best means of reaching your objectives, remembering that how *well* you set your plans will determine how *far* you get.

When it comes to personal goals, many young people fail to give them enough thought. Take, for instance, the matter of deciding where to live. Most young people want to live away from home, on their own. It means independence, it is freedom, but it is also expensive. Your budget must be able to afford it. If it does not, what are the alternatives? Logically, presuming it's okay with the parents, one obvious one is to remain living at home. The cost is usually minimal, especially if the parents understand that the young person is trying to save money. But are there disadvantages which would require flexibility and compromise by both sides? Probably. These would need to be weighed well and discussed beforehand. For example, would there be flak over late hours? Could Springsteen be played above a whisper? Would friends be free to visit and party? What chores might be expected in lieu of rent?

If your budget can afford it, without doubt, there is a special satisfaction in striking out on one's own, away from all parental jurisprudence. If living quarters are to be shared with friends, however, the choice of roommates is an issue that should also be addressed. One person might be a lot of fun to party with, but just too flaky or irresponsible to live with on a daily basis; another's morals might offend your standards; another's habits or ways might be too lazy or too rigid ever to become compatible with yours, and so on.

Impulsive decisions on where you live can lead to a lot of

unnecessary, embarrassing, or sticky predicaments, so give your future accommodation a lot of thought before you move in. Try always to make it "home," a place to which you want to return every night.

Buying a car, vacationing in Hawaii, purchasing a diamond ring or a beautiful painting, are other personal goals that require a good amount of prudent foresight. To undertake any of them without bankrupting yourself is the challenge, and all such challenges entail pre-planning.

Your career aim, I know, is to be a top sales executive. Toward that end, you have already set—and met—some mighty fine objectives. You score high marks consistently in the business courses you are pursuing at university. But what happens after that? You cannot say, because, although you have mastered the setting and planning of short-term goals, no thought has yet been given the long-term. It is high time to start planning for them.

Pinpoint the date you wish to reach your summit – ten, twelve years from now? There are plateaus that must be crossed en route to that peak. Chart them, and allot each a realistic target date on your mental calendar. For instance, your first goal is to find a suitable sales job; your second will probably be a sales manager's position six or seven years hence. Tag it with a date, and then carefully think out every step it will take to get you there: the annual sales quotas *you* set for yourself, the series of after-hour business courses you can squeeze into your schedule, talking to sales managers for some valuable firsthand insight about what their jobs entail, etc. – and then – *go for it.*

That, above all, is what Johnny has learned to do. Consistently, he has sighted his bullseyes, aimed carefully and painstakingly each time, and then courageously fired. His record of fine accomplishments tells the rest of the story, but it would be incomplete indeed, if we overlooked another major facet of his many strengths: his determination to overcome failures.

Undoubtedly, as Robert Burns observed, even the best-laid plans of mice and men often go astray. Failures befall us. You have encountered a few minor ones along your way, but nothing yet that anyone could term a major setback. What we do about those disappointments separates the men (and the women) from the mice – whether we keep on slugging after a big failure, or give up and play dead.

A great many people only dream of their goals; others lay out their plans and start carrying them out only to stop the moment a hitch interrupts them. It is here we lose most of our would-be winners – when all the pieces do not come together as planned, and no effort is made to recoup, revamp, or to try again. Sometimes the going does get *damn* tough, but think of Thomas Edison at such times: he failed *thousands* of times in his experiments before he perfected the light bulb. Persistent? Stubborn? I'd say he was! But that's what it takes, dear daughter, to make dreams come true. You will make yours come true, if you treat your failures as challenges and remember that they play a big part in the winning game. There would be no victories if there were no battles to fight.

I see that spunk, that creative persistence, in Johnny, and I see it in you. And just as your eyes sparkle over Johnny's achievements, so do mine glow with pride over yours. Keep on tapping your potential and creating a life of great worth.

Much love,

A Fellow Goal-Setter

7 Day One

Dear Rookie:

You've landed your first job! My heartiest congratulations. It's a great achievement. Perhaps you are thinking "*not* so great" because, after all, the company *is* owned by your father. Hard-nosed as this might sound–daughter or no daughter, you would not have been hired had there been any doubt about your ability. Our success was built around smart, hard working, and dedicated people. You would not have been allowed to join this select group had you not convinced our management that you were made of the same cloth and that you could do the job.

My only directive to your management was that a good training program be laid out for you and a fair probationary period be set, after which they determine either the continuance–or cancellation–of your employment with us. But that is the same message I have imparted to all of our senior people on the hirings or firings of all our personnel. So you were accorded no special favours there.

I will admit you are correct that, as my daughter, you will at first be more closely observed and scrutinized by the rest of the staff than are most of our new employees. It is up to you to give your colleagues as little as possible to criticize about you. Neglect none of the basics such as good grooming, good manners, getting to work on time, and being cooperative with and considerate of your fellow workers.

Putting what you have learned academically into practice will only require patience and time. During that time, you will more and more comprehend the value of working hard. For most of us mere mortals, it is the only route we know to success. But I caution you again to remind yourself constantly of your long-term goals and of the absolute need to keep steering your effort in that direction. And I caution you to treat routine and repetitive work not as an impediment to your progress, but as the essential *experience* you will need to help you reach your summit. It is usually the tallest cliff that needs climbing en route.

Among the other tall cliffs you may face is one called *sexism* – the discrimination or oppression of women by men on the basis of sex. A great many men have known all along, or have learned by now, that their best progress is made by accurately measuring an employee's ability, effort, and intelligence regardless of gender. Regrettably, though, as unfair and costly a deficiency as it is, sexism is still practised – however covertly or even unintentionally – by many other men in business.

It is clear that women have won the right to take full part in business life. There are far more women in jobs like yours and even in more senior, executive positions than was dreamed possible only twenty-five years ago. However, from time to time, these women do encounter male colleagues or clients who have not accepted women's presence in decision-making positions. There are many instances, ranging from the blatant to the subtle, that indicate that a woman is not being taken seriously – and you should watch out for them. Let me give you a few such scenarios.

As one of our sales people, you will, of course, be calling on many of our present or prospective clients. Some of your male customers may not readily accept you or your advice and might ask to deal with your manager or with some other man "in authority." Politely, get it across that you were assigned the account and insist that they deal with you. Then inform your manager of the action you took. (It will be a good test of *his* position on the subject and, let's hope, he will pull out all stops to assist you.)

You might find out that matters undoubtedly under your realm of responsibility are being decided by others behind your back. The classic example of this is that of the "boys" neglecting to invite you along to a lunch where your business is being discussed. Because such parleys are usually informal, they will be that much harder for you to find out about. As soon as you do, however, you should politely point out and insist that, if you are accountable for the work being discussed, you should be included as part of the decision team on all occasions. Otherwise your position will be undermined and your development seriously hampered.

In all your meetings with colleagues, management, or clients, you should not only ensure that your presentations and interventions are clear and compelling, but that they are *being listened to*. All too often, to my unending dismay at the high cost of the folly, some men have a way of "tuning out" a woman's opinion. Therefore, ask for comment at the time of your presentations. Do not wait for it to be offered, for it may never come. It's known as the "cold shoulder treatment" – a costly detriment to the company, to your job, and quite possibly to the perpetrator's own position down the road.

There are two other common forms of discrimination. One situation which many a woman faces is finding out that a male colleague who does essentially the same work and carries the same amount of responsibility is being paid considerably more than she. The other is that of being passed over for promotion in favour of a man no more qualified than she. Either circumstance certainly calls for a satisfactory explanation by the man-

49

ager, and no one should feel shy about asking for it. If the manager's rationale is inadequate or smacks of chauvinism, more senior management should be asked for answers.

By the way, there is no harm in letting your bosses or your colleagues (male or female) know when you are angry about some aspect of your work. But make sure they know that you are *angry* not *upset*. The first is considered a rational response; the second, irrational and immature. Stands to reason: Ranting or raving over an issue will only cause your listener to dismiss your argument as an emotional outburst instead of giving its content the deliberation it likely deserves.

I have no doubt that, in time, you will be in a senior position, working with male subordinates. Some might have difficulty working for a female boss. Hold a private meeting with any who do and get it out in the open. Tell them you expect their resentment to cease. If it does not, you should fire them, not transfer them, as your last resort, or they may never learn.

I stress again, however, you must maintain calmness and decorum during any such confrontation. You are in the forefront of a revolution within the business world, which was exclusively male terrain until only thirty years ago. With time, sexism will be almost entirely obliterated, but I dare say that there will always be some die-hard chauvinists – male and female – who will never change their narrow-minded prejudices; who will never overcome their resentment of the presence of the opposite sex in the work place. And, without doubt, they will remain in the outer fringes of the spectrum where the vast majority of us are prospering.

Outdated sexism, including its most frivolous forms, has convinced many business women in recent years that they would be much better off starting their own businesses than trying to prove themselves in some of our larger enterprises. There is no doubt in my mind that these new businesses will prosper. As a matter of fact, I saw a recent study in our country which concluded that over half of all new businesses are now being created by women – and that the survival rate of these new ventures during the early years exceeds that of new businesses started by men!

I am sorry if some of the foregoing made heavy reading for you only a few days before you start your first job, but it would have been remiss of me not to touch on this subject at this juncture to try to prepare you for some of the jaundice you might have soon to contend with. Let me quickly add, however, that having "studied" you for over twenty years now, I know whereof I speak when I assure you that you have the brains, the drive, the courage, the spirit, the personality, the tenacity, and every other inner resource you might have to draw on, to catch any shining star you set your sights on.

So go for it, Tiger!

Love,

On-Ward

8 Love
and Marriage

My Dear Starry-eyed Daughter:

Forgive my laughter the other day when you asked if I knew that you were in love with Mark. It struck me as a hilarious question only because it has been so vividly obvious the last few months that even our canary couldn't have missed it. When a person walks around a house glowing and lit up like a Christmas tree as you have been lately, one would have to be pretty dumb not to figure out the reason why.

But your joy is heartwarming, even though, as you confided, this great wave of emotion which has come over you has you scared half to death. Don't let it frighten you unduly. It is a common phenomenon. Risking an overuse of metaphors, let me try to explain your bewilderingly delirious condition this way: Love is an attraction that has grown to the stature of a gigantic mountain—beautiful, majestic, incomparably thrilling; it is the greatest, most powerful, and most desireable of all human emotions. It endures throughout the world, often a silent missionary carrying balm for the severest of wounds or disputes between people. Where there is love, there is kindness, charity, understanding, and hope.

As young people, quite naturally, we become greatly preoccupied with feelings of love for a particular person and with thoughts of marriage. It is a universal drive; a mating urge, if you wish. We fantasize our ideal partners and dream of living happily together forever after. But "forever after" must be seen as a reality, not as unending romance. Too often, couples jump into marriage for the wrong reasons: to get away from home, to "tie the knot" because everyone else is, or because they believe it will be a perennial state of heavenly bliss and ecstasy. It is not. Any marriage has its share of hardships. But it will be an unending source of happiness and a haven against the world if, during the rough times, there is enough love to overcome all.

John Phillips Marquand quipped, "Marriage . . . is a damnably serious business, particularly around Boston." Whether it is more serious around Boston I do not know, but I do indeed consider marriage a union that should not be entered into frivolously anywhere. And if you are thinking of marriage, I would ask you most to try to assess the depth and the lasting potential of your love – and of Mark's.

Without casting aspersions on him, and with no hidden meanings behind any of my words, I think there are a few traits of any "intended" that should be appraised clearsightedly before marriage. Being in love strongly affects and often vastly alters true personalities. People under the spell sometimes change for much the better overnight. They become more kind, more considerate, more helpful, and downright more amiable than they normally are. The intensity of newfound love seems to obscure all flaws in their makeup as effectively as does ivy on a ramshackle wall. But just as ivy wilts in time, so do sham virtues when the first rush of heady emotions begins to subside. It happens all too often. What we thought was, wasn't, isn't, and never will be. It comes as a rude shock and becomes increasingly more difficult to deal with if the personality that emerges from behind the facade is a lot less agreeable than the facade had promised. For this reason, most parents urge their children to take enough time to get to know their prospective partners really well before they embrace matrimony.

Perhaps it is asking a lot of one walking on clouds to try to see through them, but in truth, I do not believe that it should be all that hard to sum up the predominant nature of a person with whom you are spending a great deal of your time. All it takes is a pair of eyes and a couple of ears wide open at least half the time. Is your loved one generous toward his fellow man, or is he stingy with his time and interest in them, or with his money? Does he like the world in general, or does he hate much of what he sees? Is there a lack of truthfulness in him? Does he "use" other people? Has he pride in his job, or is he frequently absent from work and uncommitted to it? Socially, is he courteous and conversationally able, or a bumpkin? What is he like when he has had too much to drink?

Am I looking, in fatherly fashion, for some superman for you who doesn't exist? No. Only hoping that you will share your magnificence with a super human being–and not co-exist with someone a lot less than fine.

Madáme de Staël, hundreds of years ago, concluded that, "Love is the whole history of a woman's life. It is but an episode in a man's." Lord help all marriages if she was right!

Not so many years ago, George Bernard Shaw penned this funny/sad commentary on the topic: "When two people are under the influence of the most violent, most insane, most delusive, and most transient of passions, they are required to swear that they will remain in that excited, abnormal, and exhausting condition continuously until death do them part."

Needless to say, I am not at all as cynical about the subject as either of these two writers. However, there is no doubt that something is very wrong these days when one out of every three of our marriages fails. This is a tragic statistic. Divorce is difficult enough when no children are involved; absolute agony when they are. I have shared a little of the anguish several of my friends endured during and after their divorces. My heart would cry if you ever had to withstand the same. Peering through those frothy clouds now and then for a clear-eyed view of your prospective bridegroom is good insurance against its happening to you.

In time, both your and your husband's geyser of love will subside to a less "insane, delusive, transient, abnormal, exhausting" passion or condition than Shaw speaks of, and to an exquisitely deep and constant emotion. But never will it diminish to the "episode" of de Staël's description if you both consciously and daily strengthen the bond between you with tenderness, kindness, understanding, respect, and truth.

The principle of sharing will govern most every detail of your married life, for no longer will either of you be walking alone, but as half of a pair. Virtually everything you do will have some minor or major effect on the other. But I hasten to add that the togetherness of a good marriage should never be allowed to become *smothering*. There must always be room for individuality and the enjoyment or pursuit of singular interests. If your favorite sport is tennis and his is baseball, allow some space for the separate pastimes. That includes an occasional fishing trip with the guys for him or an out-of-town excursion with the girls for you: "Absence makes the heart grow fonder," said Propertuis around 10 B.C., but I would caution – only in small doses, for there is also an old refrain that goes, "When I'm not near the one I love, I love the one I'm near!" Need I say more?

Marriage is the deepest kind of friendship. Measure carefully your selection of a lifelong partner and friend. A kind, honourable, and generous man is worth a hundred or more handsome or rich men without these qualities. Never mistake "bonuses" for traits of any person.

As a father, I desire a son-in-law who will love my daughter truly and deeply, who will treat her gently, and who will be her mightiest ally, her greatest love, and her most trusted confidant and helpmate all her life.

I repeat, not a *superman*—just a super human being.

Love,

Another of Your Admirers

P.S. If you have further interest in my observations on this topic, please read the letter I wrote your brother entitled "Marriage," just reversing the sexes.

9 Hard Work

Dear Debater:

That was quite a discussion we had at the dinner table last night. Though the rafters were shaking, I was fascinated by your and your brother's varying views about why some people are successful in business while some are not. Since (as often is the case when you and your brother "get going" lately) there was little chance of wedging in a few comments of my own on the topic, I thought I would do so now – calmly, alone in my library, and after having given both your contentions some *quiet* contemplation.

There are, of course, a great number of factors that come into play, most of which the two of you mentioned, such as a good or tepid education, an upbeat or downer attitude, a winning or a just "so-so" personality, a belief in oneself or uncertainty, courage or timidity, and so on. But it seems to me that you both gave the ingredient of *hard work* rather short shrift in your heated exchange. Oh yes, it was alluded to as a component of success, but I must say that you both left me wondering whether either of you has yet given this item enough serious thought. I would, if I were you, for some very important reasons.

Many people work hard all their lives and do not get very far in business probably because of a shortage of too many of the good traits you mentioned last night. Some people still manage to achieve success even though they lack a few, or even a lot of these qualities – but I can tell you that *no one* succeeds who does not work hard enough during the early stages of career-building.

As you will recall (heartless as it is of me to bring it up again), your marks during your first year of university were horribly disappointing. Why? Because you were more interested in other things, such as exploring your new freedom, and partying, and boys, than you were in your classes. And fair enough! You are only human, and the mistake you made is common to a great many first-year university students. In your case, you were most fortunate that it did not cost you the year, and that in your second year, when interest in your future had become paramount again, you were able to catch up with your studies and earn the marks to prove it.

In the business world, you must gauge your level of interest in various lines of work very carefully, for, just as it was in university, the less interest you have in what you are doing, the less inclined you will feel to work hard, and the slower will be your progress. A person whose interest in her work is very high will likely work at least 50 per cent more than the required forty hours per week, and she will feel far less fatigue than one who puts in her forty hours, frustrated, or bored to the eyeballs by her job. Indeed, I know many people who work *seventy* hours a week – or more – without a hint of tiredness. They love what they are doing; some, so much so, that they joke how guilty they feel about getting paid for doing it. That is because their keen interest in their work has turned it into a labour of love.

Many people prefer anything else over work – the TV set, shopping, sitting around a bar, or sitting around doing nothing. It is not hard to figure out how far their interests will take them. However, there are things in life far more important to many people than success in the workplace – and I have no quarrel with them. But for you, with your great desire for success, you had better make sure that you are far more interested in work than you are in play over the next number of years. Success does not come to those who are not willing to work their butts off for it, if they have to. You have the time (everyone does), but you must have the interest, the willingness, and the fortitude too. Thomas Edison, along with his many brilliant inventions, left behind this crisp summation: "There is no substitute for hard work." Simple, to the point, and very true.

As you know, a country's greatest resource is its people. In countries that prosper, the work ethic is very high, and there is great individual belief in and commitment to going as far as your abilities will take you. That is what is needed to keep a country strong; it is what is needed to keep a business strong; and it is what is absolutely essential if you wish to attain success: the willingness, the desire, and the determination to go as far as your abilities will take you.

The advantages of hard work include the special happinesses that come from achieving, from savouring the respect of others and – more important – of self, from experiencing the personal pride of clearing your own path in this world, and from feeling as vital a part of creation as are the elements themselves.

I have absolutely no respect for anyone who, while able to better himself, is just too damn lazy to try. Nor have I any for those who, while blessed with a God-given ability to aid society, only take from it instead. They are the *poachers* of this world – and the saddest thing is that they are swindling themselves most severely, without even knowing it. In my books, getting away with doing as little work as possible is getting away with *nothing*, for it leads nowhere; to no personal advancement, no professional advancement, no betterment of any kind. Surely, not one of us was put on this earth for the purpose of promoting nothingness.

Your grandmother, whose work week consisted of a solid eighty hours, was in complete accord with Horace of centuries past who said, ''Life grants nothing to us mortals without hard work.'' I hope the next time you and your brother debate the prime requisites of success, you both concede that Grammy and Horace knew of what they spoke, and you slot *hard work* very near the top of your respective lists.

Love,

The Referee

10 Matching the

Company's Growth

Dear Julie:

You were shocked to learn of my decision to promote Mr Fenton over Mr Robarts to the position of vice-president of operations the other day. You might also be surprised to hear that my final decision did not hinge on their respective experience or capabilities, which are quite equal in my opinion, but on the extent of their active commitment to keep growing with our companies *through continued learning*. Let me elaborate on this.

You know how pleased I was to hear you had enrolled in a new business course recently. I was pleased for many reasons. Your interest in learning is intact. I have noticed that many of your friends, having finished school, now feel that that was enough learning effort to exert in order to secure their future and keep bread on their table; their destinies are pat. It is simply not so. There is no measure of the value of continued education in one's personal and professional life, and it is a fact that many ignore when they complain about not getting ahead in life, or that life is the pits, or that it is so boring that they hate getting up in the mornings. In business, it is a cardinal rule that you must continually keep learning if you want to succeed. The more knowledge you acquire, the greater you can expect your success to be.

In general, people move up the corporate ladder as they gain experience and, in general, very few cite more than their experience when seeking promotion. But watch that person progress who gives management both experience and an active pursuit of self-betterment programs to consider: the person studying new and innovative techniques outside of a nine-to-five work day to improve current skills or business performance. By using part of the other one hundred and twenty-eight hours in a week – even if only two or three – to hone skills or professional knowledge, he cannot help but stand out above all competitors who do not. He will be the one promoted ahead of them all, and the more knowledge he continues gaining in his area of expertise, the increasingly more valuable he will become to the company.

But you know who *really* catches my eye? The person who not only enrolls in courses pertinent to his own sphere of business, but in those relevant to other departments, as well. There are financial and marketing aspects to every business, of course, and usually there is personnel management, production, and often such specialized areas as those connected with the buying or selling of businesses, or with income tax regulations, or with patent law. The list is long. The person who invests time learning as much as she can about as many of them as she can is making a big investment in her future. There is always great wonderment expressed over this or that amazing executive's rapid rise up the corporate ranks. Dollars to doughnuts, it is almost always a person who spends a great deal of her non-office hours boning up on as many facets of business as her brain can absorb; a compulsive learner with an insatiable appetite for knowledge.

Based on an opinion poll of but one, mine, I would wager

that no more than one person out of a hundred pursues learning – even a minute beyond regular working hours – about their chosen fields of work. So you can see how easy I think it is, through a series of well-thought-out and constructive study programs, to outdistance most contenders for the laurel wreath you want to claim. Note that I said, "through a series of well-thought-out and constructive study programs," for as wise Confucius discerned, "learning without thought is labour lost; thought without learning is perilous." Furthermore, you must stick to your programs over many, many years – if not for an entire lifetime. I am in my autumnal years, and I still feel a great need of further learning not only to outdistance my competitors, but to maintain steady footing on the rung of that "ladder" I have managed thus far to ascend.

Ponder this. The growth of any society first depends, of course, on the ability of its people to read and write its own language correctly. In our country, and in a considerable number of other western countries, there is a high dropout rate among high school students. Coupling that with the fact that a huge number of our high school *graduates* are functionally illiterate – lacking basic language skills – is cause for alarm. Great alarm, for it means that we are losing the most valuable of all resources: an educated people.

There is universal marvel over Japan's extraordinary progress as a nation over the past forty years. But can there be any mystery involved in its phenomenal growth, especially in recent years, when you contemplate the fact that 95 per cent of its high school students graduate at an educational level equivalent to first or second year of college in most western societies? And this country's strongest of all resources, an educated and hard-working citizenry, cannot help but pay even bigger dividends in the future, for such a combination constitutes a powerful one-two punch for world prominence.

For our country's fine standard of living to survive, today's galloping technological changes and advancements demand a well-educated people. Bring this thought closer to home. If you and the rest of our work force are not encouraged to keep in touch with these rapid changes by pursuing personal continued education programs, how will our businesses survive? The answer is simple: they will not. Only those companies who successfully implement ways and means of continuously educating their work forces will continue to prosper. The same principle that applies to countries, applies to companies. As management, you had better heed it, or, once I'm gone, you will be coming to visit my gravesite in a go-cart instead of a Lincoln. Guard against your company's growth ever overtaking your personal managerial growth. As the company expands, so must your administrative skills, else you will join the ranks of the many fired or side-lined executives who also failed to wake up and smell the smoke in time.

As well as studying your business courses and reading and learning as much as you can about business in general, include some subjects of a personal nature in your self-improvement curriculum. For instance, and as I have already told you, I believe there is enormous personal benefit to be gained by studying the workings of the human mind. It irks me to no end that I only began acquiring knowledge of such vital import in my fifties instead of my twenties. Please do not yourself miss the golden opportunity of profiting by it now; at least, do not let another day go by without opening one of the books in my collection on the subject and testing the validity of my advice.

At your fingertips in every library or bookstore are mountains of self-help books on themes ranging from how to maintain great health to how to unfold your napkin just so at a dinner party. I advocate reading history as another excellent means of bettering one's understanding of life; studying how our forebears coped with and overcame ordinary and extraordinary circumstances, challenges, or conquests. Many events in life are repeats, and many of the ''how to's'' we seek have already been tried and proved by others – and they are all there for the sharing, between the covers of a book. So are many of their mistakes, which should teach us how to avoid making the same.

I hope the rewarding outcome of your first course will spur you to enroll in more and more until learning becomes an addiction for you and that, in the words of Laurence Sterne, "The desire for knowledge, like thirst of riches, increases ever with the acquisition of it." Forty hours at the office and five hours of learning leaves one hundred and twenty-three hours a week for sleeping, eating, and fun. Think about that. And never forget that your value to us in our businesses will grow in direct proportion with the degree of attention and perseverance you give this matter.

In a decade from now, you will be ten years older and that much smarter, or you will just be ten years older. Do not repeat Mr Robarts' mistake by choosing the latter objective.

Affectionately,

D. K. Sotolar

11 Be Decisive

My Dear Julie:

I was sorry to learn that you lost out on your bid for the distribution rights to the new European line of chemicals. This product line would have been a nice bonus for our company. However, I was even sorrier to learn the circumstances under which we lost out. Seems we had a good inside track that should have taken us to the finishing line first, but we blew it in the home stretch by your not making a vital decision fast enough.

Perhaps you can say in your defence that no one had told you how anxious the European company was to appoint an agency in our country, and that you thought you had more time to make the required decision. Well, you can say it, but I won't buy it.

One of the costliest flaws of many people involved in the business world is the inability to make prompt decisions. The waste and inefficiency of sluggish decision-making costs a company dearly if it is allowed to proliferate. It is called *procrastination*, and I deplore it.

In this case, you had all the facts you needed beforehand, but you didn't take the time to assess them carefully enough to allow you to make a decision on the terms being offered by the European company. You should have taken the time. Edward Young of long ago stated, "Procrastination is the thief of time." Indeed, such was the thief that stole your long-hoped-for new distributorship.

There is no pat formula for success in business, but there are a few known and time-proven essentials. Being decisive is one of them. Recognizing the moment when a decision is yours and yours alone to make is another one. But even then – what matter? – if the necessary homework is not at your fingertips. Any decision-making – but most especially swift decision-making – is a challenge; the greater this challenge, more than likely, the greater the opportunity. A lot of such opportunities slip by those who hesitate too long; those who waste time worrying and fretting over the predicament instead of using it to formulate a constructive decision. Many of them have probably not heard of – or if they have, have ignored or derided – the following simple format, ages old, for arriving at an important decision.

Once all your facts are gathered and each has been evaluated as either a plus or a minus, all you need further is a blank sheet of paper, a pen, and a little more of your time. Now draw a line down the centre of your sheet and place a plus sign on the top of one side and a minus sign on the other. List your data in its corresponding column in point form. Carefully assess and then designate a value of one to ten beside each factor in your columns. Total the value of each column. One side greatly outweighing the other should provide you with a pretty clear indication which direction your decision should take or, conversely, that perhaps the entire project should be reworked or re-evaluated.

If the total score of each column is too close to be definitive, you will then need to rely on good old-fashioned intuition to see you through. But for heaven's sake, once you've accomplished all the preliminaries, take that bull by the horns and make your decision. And waste not a moment either before – *or after* – stewing about it. A decision made is a worry gone; a challenge conquered. Spice of life! It was one of Harry S. Truman's credos that once a decision is struck it should not be rethought or reworried over afterward. As much of his down-to-earth counsel was, it is sound, common-sense advice worth embracing.

The fear of failure is, of course, often the main cause of indecisiveness. But better to try and fail than to stand still passively watching opportunities fly by your office window and into your competitors'. Most emphatically, moreover, passivity has never yet an effective executive made. Neither have its pals, vascillation and hesitation. Being in business means making decisions, trying new ideas, taking chances, grabbing opportunities, winning – and losing. No champion wins all of the time, just most of the time. But, how would he ever win if fear of failure consistently prevented him from ever trying? So it is in business. One fearless baby step forward soon becomes one fearless giant step closer to the championship waiting at the other end.

Another cause of indecision is out and out, downright laziness, or the begrudging of sometimes having to put in strenuous working hours to compile information upon which effective decisions can be made. I have never perceived your being either lethargic or resentful toward your work but I must admit that I have sometimes wondered why your desk is so often obscured from sight by an avalanche of paper. Wouldn't an extra hour in the morning every now and then, before everyone else comes in, and before the telephones, telexes, and fax machines start their disruptive clanging, lighten that backlog considerably? I think it would, and I suggest you try it.

Incidentally, as in favour of prompt decision-making as I sound and as I most assuredly am, I am equally in favour of reversing a decision as soon as it becomes judiciously possible once it has been proven wrong. Going the wrong way on a one way street in business not only becomes the more demoralizing, but also the more expensive, the further along you go. Best to U-turn on such occasions, just as fast as you safely can.

This epistle would not be complete without a word or two about some select circumstances which seem to call for a propitious lapse of time – a period of "aging," if you will, of facts or figures, testings, or so on, before a decision is struck. Delaying a decision in such cases is only right, of course, provided you have made a conscious decision to postpone making a decision. This is still decision-making and not procrastination, and there is a vast difference between the two.

I know you feel badly over the loss of this prospective new agency, and I suspect that you are not feeling much better now having read this letter. What I know that you don't know, however, is that although not right now, and perhaps not tomorrow, but very shortly, you will be regarding this loss as a major gain in your life. Why so? Because it has so well served to prove the value of nurturing decisiveness among the many other sterling qualities of your character. It has been a harsh lesson, I know, but I also know that by its very severity it will broaden the scope and sweeten the elation over your very next success. I feel very good about that for there are lots of bigger fish for you to catch out there than the one that got away this time.

Go reel them in, Baby!

Love,

The Chairman of the Board

12 Good Deeds

My Kind and Caring Daughter:

What a pleasure it was the other day to hear by chance through your friend, Kate, that you have joined the "Adopt a Grandparent" program in our city. I had heard of this excellent program, which encourages young people to visit our institutionalized elderly, but had no idea that you were already among its active participants. It is such a shame that we all hear too little of such kind acts as this and the many other that occur daily throughout the world. The media seem to play up "doom and gloom" stories – those of people hurting people – and downplay those of people helping people. I would certainly much rather hear more about the latter but, as they say, that's not what sells newspapers.

It makes a person feel so good to perform an act of kindness that I find it strange that more people do not practise it more often. Many find themselves too embarrassed to go out of their way to help someone, especially if he is a stranger. Too few of us give a guy a helping hand with a flat tire, help an old person cross the street, give someone else our seat on a bus or a street-car. It should be the other way around, of course: We should be embarrassed when we fail to help when it is needed.

I don't know if you have yet observed that those who instinctively offer help to anyone else when it is needed are seldom left in the lurch themselves in times of trouble; some-one, as if by magic, is always there for them, too, to "return in kind." But there is no magic to it at all, for one good deed always generates another; good attracts good. It is one of the most pow-erful chain reactions in the world–and each of us has the power to set off at least several such charges each day of our existence. We don't have to look far for people who could use some form of assistance. Virtually everyone has someone as near as next door who needs perhaps only a comforting word or a small action to help get them through the day. There are the elderly, the poor, the shut-ins, and the disabled – all of whom we live among and often forget about entirely or deliberately ignore.

On the topic of "helping thy neighbour," your grand-mother told me about a remarkable young woman who lived in her farming community. The girl had seldom been accepted by anyone in the area; perhaps she had some faults, I don't know. In any case, her husband died very young, leaving her to raise four children all alone from the resources of an extremely meagre farm. She worked dawn to midnight keeping that family going.

The old farmer who lived alone next door was stricken with cancer and became bedridden. Only this one neighbour, as busy as she was, could find any time at all to look after him. She nursed him for a year before the old fellow died. Immedi-ately, the relatives lined up at the lawyer's office. It was to be a great day for them, for rumour had spread that the old boy, although he had lived very frugally, had somehow acquired a considerable sum of money during his lifetime and now, nat-urally, they figured it would all be theirs. But not a penny did they get. There were howls of anguish when the lawyer announced that all the money, the farm, and some other property owned by the deceased had all been bequeathed to the young woman who had nursed him during his illness. He had known how hard it had been for her; that hers had not been an easy, one-time act of compassion, but a gruelling schedule of day-to-day care-giving.

Needless to say, this lady's life changed overnight for she no longer had to struggle to feed her young brood and herself. But something else happened too, which meant almost as much to her: No longer was she being shunned or scorned by the community. By his last act, the old farmer had brought her goodness and the task she had accomplished to light, for which, of course, she was admired and respected by all. (Perhaps even by the old gentleman's relatives – if they ever got over the shock of being left out of his will.)

Seldom, though, are the rewards of performing good deeds either as dramatic or publicly admired as in this story. And that is as it should be, for the true reward of aiding, or sharing, or giving should be that very quiet, *personal* knowledge that you've just done something that makes you a little better person for it; that makes you like yourself a little better. To me, wanting or needing to be thanked or publicly acknowledged for any good we do, waters down the sincerity of our actions. Countless people provide vast amounts of time, energy, or money to various causes anonymously, probably for that very reason. They need no thanks, no publicity, only the satisfaction that they've set off a few more of those powerful chain reactions I mentioned earlier that "return in kind."

In my view, the other unsung heroes of our times are the legions of people who give freely of their time for the betterment of our society. In the health-care field alone, there are volunteers at hospitals and nursing institutions, fund-raisers for many societies of medical research into such illnesses as cancer, arthritis, heart and kidney disease, and so on. In education there are those who help establish scholarship grants and gifts to young people who could not attain an education otherwise. Most of them are seldom commended for their efforts publicly or with

75

a lot of hoop-la. They just do what needs to be done where and when it needs doing with no expectation other than that their effort will help someone who needs it and the joy of re-experiencing that glow they feel each time they give more of themselves. It is the same glow I see on your face each time you receive a communication from or about Fatoumata Traore, the young girl in Mali, Africa, whom you adopted as a foster child through the Canadian Foster Parents' Plan. I only found out about this venture of yours some six months after you had pledged your support, but I will never forget the pride and esteem I felt for you the day I learned about it. Asking for no one's advice, seeking no accolades, motivated only by the generosity of your heart, you took on this monthly commitment on a salary that could still barely afford it. Which brings me to another observation on the topic at hand.

I think it entirely possible that the noblest of deeds are those we undertake during the most difficult of personal circumstances. In other words, when we console when we most need consolation, ease pain when we ourselves are aching, or when we give or share when we can least afford it, these efforts are the worthiest of all our actions.

Some years ago I assisted my cardiologist in raising some funds from business associates to buy a badly needed piece of medical equipment. We had raised about $50,000 by the time a certain eighty-year-old woman heard about our efforts. She arrived at the doctor's office one day and left her old age pension cheque for that month, duly endorsed to the fund. It amounted to $185. Why am I mentioning it? Because the doctor knew of her poverty; $185 was all she had to live on for the month, but of far greater importance to her was the fact that it would help her doctor buy that piece of equipment. We could not offend our wonderful supporter by returning her cheque; we could not rob her of this noblest of all deeds. Some donors contributed upwards of $7,000 each, but I think you can guess whose donation all of us appreciated most. And none of us will ever forget the meaning of true caring and giving set for us by that beautiful old woman.

Could there be a better example for any of us that there must be something to the old adage, "It is better to give than to receive?" None that I can think of today, sweet daughter. Philip James Bailey, a nineteenth century poet wrote, "We live in deeds, not years." So keep spreading your kind heart around. I like good things happening to you in the way of "returns in kind."

Love,

Daddy

13 Emotions in Business

My Dear Daughter:

It was good to get back recently, after that extensive business trip. I love seeing the world, but nothing beats "Home, Sweet Home" to me. As always on returning, I wondered what had happened during my absence and upon reviewing your study on the prospective purchase of the SMS company, I realized a lot had happened. As this was the first time you had proposed such a venture to me, I was, of course, keenly interested in finding out what you were up to. Having now dispensed with the pleasantries, however, brace yourself, for the rest of this letter is not about to be quite as pleasant.

The prospect of buying a company, without doubt, is a wonderfully exciting, exhilarating experience. It conjures visions of empires, power beyond measure, and it plants a smile on one's face, which broadens as the profit figures magically mount on the fantasy income statement. Having romped among the same clouds on several occasions myself in the past, please believe me, I understand the feeling. The hard truth of the matter is, though, that I have learned the hard way to now view each proposed new acquisition as one would contemplate crossing a minefield: with great care, for I have been blown up a few times.

The rationale you have given as our main reason for purchasing this company seems to rest heavily on the fact that it would make us one of the largest companies in our field of industry. That is certainly a mighty fine goal and one which, naturally, I have strived to achieve all my business life. However, setting the goal is one thing; mapping a careful route that is sure to get us there, is another.

My biggest concern about your proposal is that you have charted only our throwing in a ton of money as your means of getting us to your destination. There seems to be a lack of measurement of the relative cost, limited consideration of their conformity with our existing business, virtually no assessment of what management would be required, almost no review of the strength of their products in the marketplace, and absolutely no answer to the question, "Why do they want to sell?" (Which leads me to suspect that your ton of money might be their biggest incentive.) Possibly, just possibly, have you lost patience with building our company to become the biggest in the marketplace by expanding yearly, but safely, at a controlled pace of growth, and that, instead, you just want size *overnight*? Possibly, just possibly, have you allowed such a daydream to become an actual challenge – and a burning one, at that?

You had not done all the homework I just mentioned, so our bank manager had nothing more to go on than I when you approached him with your proposal. He said he did not like the deal you presented to him and that it was going to cost too much money. Getting turned down by a bank manager always gets my ire up, since on such occasions they do tend to appear as Lord God Almighties pronouncing judgements on our proposals. Moreover, I always come away from the bank manager's office after being turned down feeling a little stupid. But, so I should – when I simmer down enough to acknowledge that I had been turned down either because of my own incorrect appraisal of the proposition, or because I had glossed over or missed some key considerations, or because I had not prepared my case carefully, thoroughly, and forcefully enough. Which brings me to my next point: Over the years, I have learned to esteem and heed my bank manager's experienced opinion and advice, for he has saved me a great deal of money by recommending against or for proposals such as yours.

But, I am afraid you are reacting much as I used to in my early years when my emotions would drive me to a state of near frenzy at the thought of that bank manager's audacity in trying to inhibit what I wanted to do. And I am not surprised to learn that you intend marching down the street to the next banker's office with your proposal. There is nothing wrong with finding out what our bank's competition have to offer – but not for reasons of blind anger, imagined insult, and injured ego. If you allow your emotions entirely to get the better of you in this instance, we might end up with two most unsatisfactory situations on our hands: a bad buy of a new company, and an estranged banker with whom I have built up ten years of money marriage. So let's "cool out" a little, back up, and reassess the proposal.

Your idea of buying this particular company might have merit but any evaluation of the purchase must be conducted on the basis of cold unemotional logic; careful realistic assessment of the various categories mentioned earlier, and of the company's compatability with our present operations.

Building onto business can be perilous; many an unfortunate person has built a fine business and lost it or watched it fade into oblivion because *emotion*, in the guise of ego or greed, was allowed to override rational thinking somewhere along the line. Impulsive firing of good employees, screaming at valuable suppliers, incorrect promotions, bad investments in new ventures, and avoiding customers who are difficult to deal with, are only a few examples of business misdemeanours primarily fuelled by emotion. I would like to have a nickel for every business action that is based on 90 per cent emotion and 10 per cent cold hard business logic. I'd be the richest man in town.

Keeping emotions out of business decisions can be extremely difficult at times, but it is imperative to set them aside during your deliberations. Be especially on guard when spur-of-the-moment decisions are called for. Move with dispatch, but not so rapidly that your heart and not your head resolves the issue at stake. Take that moment beforehand to ask yourself, "Does this make business sense, or am I doing this mostly for some emotionally satisfying reason?" When you no longer need to ask yourself that question, you will have become a seasoned executive.

Through experience, you will learn that earth-shaking events will continually occur in business causing your spirits to want either to soar or to plummet during decision-making times. By holding them in rein, you will increase tremendously your odds of maintaining success.

I would now suggest that you go back to the drawing board and make an in-depth study of your proposed purchase from a hard core, factual viewpoint and then, perhaps, you might want to take another go at our banker. Should these efforts lead to our buying this business *and* at a good price, then just watch my own emotions rise to meet the happy occasion.

Love,

Ironside

14 The Fine Art
of Negotiation

Dear Daughter:

Thank you for your compliment on my having obtained that
new contract for us with the American firm. The acquisition
was not without its moments of frustration but, all in all, if I
may say so myself, it was a rather good example of applying
the basic techniques of negotiation.

On the way home, I kept thinking to myself how much our
businesses depend on our utilizing the tenets of mediation. We
perform them routinely, yet seldom do we sit back and assess
exactly what they are. We negotiate with customers, employees, suppliers, banks, real-estate agents, and whether we realize
it or not, between ourselves. The ability to parley effectively is
one of our most important business skills. Why are some people
more adept than others in this important area of business? I
believe I can capsulize my opinion in a simple formula. It is:
FLEXIBILITY and EMOTION equals SUCCESS.

A person who is inflexible in his business dealings had better
have a monopoly on what he sells, for people tire of wrangling

ad nauseam and won't if there are other avenues to pursue. Flexibility is nothing more than being able to read the intensity of the other person's desire and then bending to it just as far as is needed in order to reach a successful conclusion. It's somewhat like a tree in a windstorm; it bends but seldom breaks, then stands taller than ever the day after the storm.

Now for part two of this formula: emotion. Often this is much more difficult to harness than flexibility, be it your own emotion or your adversary's. People often dig in their heels on the most ridiculous of points – usually only to prove that they are not going to be pushed around by anyone. If you need proof of this, look at how overloaded our courts and lawyers are with civil actions. Cases are backed up for months, the courts full of people who cannot negotiate agreements between themselves. One or the other side has remained inflexible, unable to suppress excess emotion or evaluate the other side's position objectively. Thus they must pay the often very high costs involved in securing the "cold neutrality of an impartial judge."

There are three rules to follow in practising the fine art of negotiation. One: Conduct a fact-finding mission. Gather all the information you can on the other party's position, and match it with your own data. Many negotiations fail right from the start because of a lack of facts. In the words of Benjamin Disraeli, "Ignorance never settles a question." Do your homework. It will ultimately make or break your case.

Two: Study the information you have culled and weigh each point on a scale of one to ten. Try to weigh the points two ways. First, define your assessment of each. Second, put on your opponent's hat and try to weigh each fact from his point of view. Understand where the other side is coming from. With enough study, you should be able to draft a chart, labelling your facts in the order of their particular importance. For example, delivery of a product might rate a two or an eight; price might range as widely on your graph, depending on the competition, your measurement of the supplier's quality, and any other factors that might come into play.

Three: divide a page in two and, from your chart, list all the negotiable points on one side and the points over which you will not budge on the other side. Keep this latter side short. List too many here, and you will have cornered yourself into an inflexible role.

You are now ready to negotiate. It might take several meetings to iron out certain issues or to provide required information over which you might want to return to your office to ponder, but nine times out of ten, your careful work will culminate in total success. When it doesn't – that one time out of ten – no doubt the muted mutterings from each side of the desk will resemble these sentiments of Heinrich Heine's: "Ordinarily he is insane, but he has lucid moments when he is only stupid." These are the impasses, by the way, during which emotion will want to steal centre stage. Make sure yours remains in check, well to the sidelines.

Another rule of successful negotiating is this: Do not put two people together to work something out who do not like one another. It portends disaster from the very start. On many an occasion I have asked the other side to please exclude a particular person from our discussions because, putting it diplomatically, our vibes clashed. People who like one another respect one another's views and opinions – and therein lies the secret to keeping emotion where it belongs in business: outside the conference room door.

Seldom, if ever, will all of your requests be met, so remember to wear your flexibility fatigues on battle day. And when you find yourself entangled in a particularly tough tug-of-war, try remembering Francois, Duc de La Rochefoucauld's words: "Quarrels would not last long if the fault were only on one side." (I keep telling your mother that, but she says it all depends from which side you're viewing the quarrel.)

Time can lend a hand, too. Sometimes there is every good reason for allowing days, weeks, or even months to pass before attempting a reconciliation or treaty. It lets the dust settle so everyone can view more clearly the issues at stake and perhaps

85

re-evaluate original conceptions or misconceptions. A time lapse allows for emotions to subside, too. More than once I have let a problem simmer on the back burner for a while, knowing that my learned colleague was doing the same. On such occasions, though, I have always tried to be the one big enough to pick up the phone first, extend an invitation for lunch, and suggest that together we try to break the deadlock between us.

Another method of resolving disputes is for both parties to select a third party to act as a mediator. An outsider can sometimes bring new perspectives to a matter or introduce some flexibility where none seems to exist. It goes without saying that such a third party must be entirely respected and trusted by both sides for such a tactic to work, and that he must have detailed knowledge of the matter at hand. For an excellent treatise on this subject, read *Conflicts* by Edward de Bono (Harrap, London, 1985). It could sharpen your negotiation skills considerably since it explains how the mind tends automatically to produce barriers during periods of dispute, and how to deal with and overcome them.

There is one additional thought to store in your mind. Situations do and will arise wherein you find yourself forced to accept the other fellow's inequitable terms. Your back will have been pushed up against a wall, and if for no reason but to clear the matter off your desk, you will find yourself settling for his biased conditions. Naturally, you will feel you lost the game at such times, and maybe you did; but my experience has been that, on the next go-round, that person did try to make amends for what he knew had been an unfair settlement. Funny how even the toughest good businessman usually has a conscience.

A note of caution: However extreme your differences might become during any of your negotiations, if it is at all possible, try never, never to allow the matter to get into the hands of the lawyers. Get all the legal advice you want while gathering your information, but only as a last recourse should you allow the courts to settle your dispute – only when you have utterly and painstakingly exhausted every other conceivable method of settlement. This is one of the toughest lessons to learn because, feeling cheated, it is only human to react impulsively, to want to take the matter to court and let the law settle it.

One man owed me $15,000 that I could not get out of him, so I sued him. My legal bills rose to $8,000, and still I kept after him. I ended up collecting not one red cent for all my efforts. My doggedness cost me $23,000 instead of the $15,000 loss I should have settled for in the first place. The reason? I had not bothered to do my homework (rule one) or it would have been clear to me right from the outset that the man just did not have the funds to pay me and was heading for bankruptcy. Emotion made a small man of me in that case.

As I look back on the incident, I now can see the even bigger blunder I made in neglecting my businesses while I kept hounding our lawyers to keep after that guy. God only knows how much it cost me, my mind bent on chasing a lost cause, instead of getting on with the businesses that were making a buck. My efforts at victory had somewhere slipped into revenge, I am ashamed to say. Please read this letter again should the same urge strike you. It will save a lot of wear and tear on your mind and on the company's pocketbook.

Love,

" Give an Inch "Ward

15 On Being
a Parent

Dear Young Mother:

Seeing your new baby yesterday filled me with enormous joy. Standing there, gazing at your beautiful new daughter, I could not help but relive the moment I first caught sight of my own firstborn – you. I thought to myself how glad I was that now you, too, are experiencing that one-of-a-kind, sublimely sweet happiness. And take it from me, it only gets better.

The initial few months, mind you, might wear you out and prove to be trying. Your new baby will not sleep when you normally sleep, she will scream her head off when she's hungry and sometimes for no apparent reason at all, and she will yell relentlessly for a diaper change. But you will cope; God gave parents an overabundance of patience just for such times. And one day, this wonderful little girl of yours will be a wonderful grownup woman beause of the love and tenderness in which I know she will constantly be enveloped by your own warm heart, and that of your husband's.

But as much as she should and, I am sure, will always feel

greatly loved by you, your new daughter will never need to feel your love more than during the first few months and years of her life. Many psychologists tell us that parental influence on their offspring is never greater than during this early period. Since your baby is helpless and totally dependent on someone else to create her sense of security, of course, it is up to you to provide it through verbally expressing your feelings for her, through holding her often and firmly, and through patiently and lovingly attending to all her needs. Never will the bond of communication between you and your child be stronger, and never will the strength of that bond be more important, for it is that which will shape her character, her well-being, and her general outlook on life.

The first six years are crucial to your success for it is during this time that the lifelong love line between parent and child is cast. And while it is a short span of years in your calendar, it is the most precarious of times in hers. Many of the very mixed-up and pathetic people of this world only got that way by living in the hell of little or no parental love, or even in fear of physical abuse by a parent.

As time goes by, there will undoubtedly be some days of anguish caused by your offspring but, mostly, there will only be days filled with even more happiness than you are experiencing right now. Among the many special thrills awaiting you is seeing your tot smile for the first time (which no one will be able to convince you was just gas), sprout her first tooth, take her first wobbly but bold step, tie her shoelaces all by herself, and meet Santa Claus in person. Besides enjoying the sheer fun and magic of all these stages, however, it is your parental duty to put a great deal of thought and effort into her upbringing.

I know that it will not be easy for you to juggle the new demands of your baby and the ongoing demands of your work during these early years. But I do know that you and your husband have created an excellent partnership and that he is as eager as you are to spend as much time as possible with his new baby. I am confident that the two of you will quickly work out a schedule that will enable you to become consummate "jugglers." Perhaps you will need to hire a babysitter or a nanny at some point so that you both can spend "quality time" with your daughter and still stay on top of your jobs.

Parents must hone their teaching skills during child-raising years and, of course, the best parents are those who teach their youngsters sound values, principles, and discipline with great patience and understanding. The lessons cannot start too early, by the way. As a matter of fact, many parents make the mistake of starting them too late, and they and their children usually pay for it somewhere down the line. "Just as the twig is bent, the tree's inclined," wrote Alexander Pope. There is a lot of truth to that.

As your young one grows, more and more will she begin to emulate many of your actions, words, and moods. You will be her role model and the all-knowing Supermom in her books for a very long time. It is a heady pinnacle parents occupy in their children's minds, involving awesome responsibilities for, without doubt, if parents lie, their children will lie; if they cheat, their children will learn how to cheat; and if they hate, their children will soon learn how to do that, too. Their minds like sponges, children absorb *everything* around them, and throughout their growing years, clearly, their parental teachings by word and example constitute a colossal portion of what they absorb and retain.

You have travelled many roads, developed an excellent character which includes many such fine traits as kindness, honesty, fairness, self-discipline, a great work ethic, a terrific sense of humour – and, of course, I could go on and on about *my* daughter as you are now carrying on about yours, but the point I am leading to is this: Who is there better to encourage, coax, and nurture the same choicest of qualities in your child, than you? There is no one better than her own parent. And when the time comes, do not entrust her major education concerning such items as sex, morals, and self-respect, or the hazards of liquor and drugs, to anyone but yourself and your husband.

How do you help your youngster steer clear of trouble? First, by carefully explaining what trouble is, and its many and varied consequences. Secondly, by maintaining her respect and love for you. If that is strong, your child will try very hard to avoid hurting you through any action which might bring down serious disappointment, shame, or disgrace upon your head. That kind of love bond started between you and your infant even before she was born, and it will grow ever stronger if you constantly express interest and support in everything she does – her school work, school activities, camp, hobbies, travel, or whatever else she might like to share with you.

Always treat your children with respect, and start talking to them about such matters as common sense, self-esteem, and being responsible as soon as they are old enough to grasp them. Discussions such as these tend to strengthen love and understanding between parent and child. But of all the virtues you might possess, forgiveness is the surest means of retaining your offspring's abiding love for you.

When a child gets into trouble, the usual stages of a parent's reaction are anger, followed by humiliation for having "exploded" over the issue, followed by the "Where did I go wrong?" blues, and ending with, "How do I repair the damage and try to bridge the gap again?" The point is, there should be but *one* stage: your taking control of the situation and resolving it. After all, you are the adult in the piece. Usually, it is fear for the youngster's safety and well being that triggers the anger parents express at such times. Keep your temper, your tongue, and your worries in check, and settle the incident rationally and calmly if you want best possible results. Your child knows she did wrong; you don't have to hammer it into her head over and over again. Rather, stress the *respect* she loses – of family, friends, and most importantly, of self – by this particular transgression. Then help her figure out how to avoid making the same mistake in the future.

Sometimes, you might want to consider bribery as a means of obtaining a desired end. Yes, I did say bribery, and I admit to having employed the tactic several times with you and your brother. The psychologists have a euphemism for bribery; they call it "positive reinforcement." In my view, the psychologists are right, for it is a way of suggesting that there are great rewards for performing well in the world. (It also gave us all a great deal of pleasure when you or your brother won some difficult goals, even if a "dangling carrot" did have something to do with it at times.) If you ever do use the ploy, use it sparingly and cautiously, only as an occasional game or challenge, and never an expected routine.

In the case of serious trouble, there might be good cause to bring in professional assistance. But however serious your child's offence might be, stand behind her at all times. Often, the deeper the trouble, the fewer the friends, and all the more need of your steadfast parental support.

When it comes to messy rooms, wet towels on the bathroom floor, uncapped tubes of toothpaste, mud tracks in the kitchen, and other minor transgressions, I hope you will recall your own younger years and not scream too loudly or too long at the kids. I have never yet met a young person who isn't perpetually guilty of all the above and more. But they are petty misdemeanors and insufficient cause for a lot of ranting and raving. As hard as it might be on some occasions, as I stressed before, do try to settle your differences with your children calmly, for rational words penetrate, and shouted words only alienate.

There are countless special delights awaiting you as a parent. I could fill volumes of the memorable moments your mother and I have enjoyed as parents of you and your brother – memories of chocolate cake all over your face on your second birthday, your brother's passion for the little treats you used to bake in your toy oven, your experimenting with Mom's makeup one day, trying on her high heels another day, his school parade, the father-daughter dance at your school, and then your first "real date" in Bermuda, and Mom and I marvelling how "grownup beautiful" you had suddenly become.

Happily, we are still sharing many such precious moments now watching you and your brother enjoying your adulthood. Perhaps one day, if Mom and I are blessed with longevity, we all four will nod our gray heads in accord as we muse:

Is this the little girl I carried?
Is this the little boy at play?
I don't remember growing older,
When did they?

When did she get to be a beauty?
When did he grow to be so tall?
Wasn't it yesterday when
they were small?

Love,

A Very Proud New Grandpa

16 Delegation

Dear Nighthawk:

The past four weeks have seen you putting in some long hours preparing an analysis of the customer services we are not fulfilling in one of our companies at present. Your report will, I am sure, tell us which of these areas can be corrected, and how. It is a study vital to the decisions we must make now in order to improve the viability of this company's future.

The preparation of a report of this magnitude should progress in five stages: one, an outline of the objective – the desired answers the report is to unfold for us; two, an examination and selection of the information required to produce the desired objective; three, the actual gathering of the required information; four, structuring of the assimilated data in a coherent manner to allow proper analysis; and five, the analysis itself, which should lead clearly to the goal set forth in the objective.

I can just hear you saying, "Well, I know all that, Daddy!" I know you do, but I am reiterating these important five stages to the preparation of a valuable report for a reason: to underscore the important role it plays in the development of an effective and successful executive. I must admit that it bothers me somewhat to see you doing all this work by yourself. When I asked you about this, your reply was that you could do it three times faster, alone, than with others trying to help you. Perhaps this is true, but the hitch in that kind of thinking is that you will still be doing this type of work, alone, ten years from now if you do not, at some point, take the trouble to teach someone else on our staff how to do it. As well, of course, should you be sick, or on holiday, or tied up with other pressing business matters when such work needs doing in short order, you will find yourself in a quandary, and more importantly, so will the company. Which brings me to the real subject of this letter: delegation.

I don't know how many times over the years people have asked me, "How do you manage to run all those companies and still leave yourself a couple of months' free time to pursue flying and the joys of Mother Nature?" My answer has always been the same: "Because I have highly competent executives looking after my businesses on a day-to-day basis." Simple answer, you say? Well, yes, it is simple, but you would be surprised how few people in business bother to train subordinates so they can turn some of their responsibilities over to them. Why so many avoid delegating tasks to the people working under them is a mystery to me. Is it lack of trust, sheer stupidity, or is the main reason, perhaps, fear that the other person might do a better job? Few are brave enough to say it, but I wish our executives knew how much I value being told a job was turned over to someone else because he or she "will probably do it better than I can." And if they say "better than you" (meaning me), I am even more enthusiastic and impressed.

I know of no faster way of improving our businesses' worth than by delegating to every willing and able body as much as he or she can handle – and then some – for as each person's work capabilities grow, so will our business grow. Conversely, stifling any deserving individual's growth is tantamount to stifling your company's growth.

Homer, about 700 B.C., had this to say about delegation: "You will certainly not be able to take the lead in all things yourself, for to one man a god has given deeds of war, and to another the dance, to another the lyre and song, and in another wide-sounding Zeus puts a good mind." To paraphrase: "Different folks, different strokes."

The first precept of sagacious delegation is a careful, in-depth assessment of your personnel's talents, ambitions, and desires. Given the chance, most people will surprise you with what they are capable of achieving. And you can bet your bottom dollar, the day they're assigned their new responsibilities, they will be walking ten feet tall. With or without a raise in salary, there is no greater thrill in business than being singled out for more challenging and stimulating work – except, perhaps, that of your satisfaction in having delegated the new roles and your observation of each person's success within them.

Now for the second precept. Permitting your staff to assume more important duties entails something you probably never thought of doing: teaching. Putting together a set of tough, competent executives and a dedicated, strong staff requires teaching them. The most successful people in business are often extremely good teachers. This includes preparing a good program, patiently allowing time for it to be digested, being supportive, and spurring your students' potential to its greatest heights.

Once you have made your selection of people and prepared your training program, the results of these efforts should be new people doing at least some of your old tasks. Now your key to ultimate success is the development of a system of control over all the realigned duties. This means establishing a method of communication between you and your personnel whereby you will be kept up to date and they will know you are on the alert for trouble and willing to correct a mistake. Above all, maintain confidence in your belief that your trainees can and will do their new jobs well. *Your* new job is to help them over the rough spots.

When you reach this level of command, you will be collecting your pay for what you are supposed to be doing. You are here to organize, lead, develop, and inspire your sales and marketing personnel and give them new challenges to tackle. You are not here to sit around either doing or supervising repetitive chores that require some, but most assuredly not all, of a good leader's time.

Having mulled over the foregoing, I cannot help but conclude that any executive who cannot or will not delegate to those under his supervision must indeed fear his own capabilities of handling his responsibilities. If that executive works for me, he has good cause to fear for his job! Each time he fails to develop another person, he succeeds in promoting dry rot in the foundations of my business. Undetected, dry rot spreads quickly and brings many a fine building toppling down, and I do not intend to allow it a foothold in any of mine!

In providing people the opportunity of proving their mettle, you are invoking one of the least understood tenets of effective leadership. One of my constant, secret, and greatest desires in business is to uncover as many bright lights hidden under bushels as I can find; to set loose untried, latent, or repressed talent of any person waiting for "a break" who, once associated with me, will try his damndest to fulfill his aspirations. I have said it before, but it is worth saying again: Build business around people, not people around business. As Virgil said way back in 50 B.C., "We are not all capable of everything."

Before you prepare your next important report, double check the five-stage process and assess which areas will require your sole input. Certainly, you must play a major role in deciding and defining the desired objective. However, what information should be obtained opens the doors to bringing in some of the other bright minds around you for their suggestions. The gathering of the actual information is a major time-consumer, so delegate this responsibility to others. The proper assimilation of the data will require close supervision by you, and the analysis will demand your careful personal review and consideration. However, here again, your subordinates' ideas and their evaluation of the data can only aid your own interpretation and, as a result, substantially reinforce your own final conclusion.

Too often, reports fail to benefit a company because they needed the talents of more than one bright mind. Get all the help you can get interpreting your information. It will lessen your personal work load immeasurably, but most important of all, by involving your people in your report, you will be making them more valuable to the company.

So – no more late nights doing what others can and should be trained to do to assist you. It will bolster both your department's strength and morale, make you look good to the boss, and the kids won't be asleep when you get home at night.

Building a business, or a department within a business, is like trying to build a pyramid – in reverse. You are the top stone. How many sturdy, supportive levels of stone eventually form the walls and foundation beneath you depends on your ability to select, train, trust, supervise, or promote the members of your work team. It's disheartening that many business executives fail to grasp this, fearing it might jeopardize their own lofty (soon to become shaky) pinnacles. I don't know about you, but I sleep well at night knowing the base of my pyramid is solid; a base of which, of course, you form a mighty cornerstone.

About 2600 B.C., in Egypt, Snefru built the first true pyramid. However, it was left to his son, Khufu, to build the ideal one, the Great Pyramid at Giza. Keep building your pyramid and like Khufu, make it the ideal one, too.

Love,

Snefru

17 On Being the Boss

Dear New Boss:

Welcome to the club! It took years of hard work, a lot of overtime hours, piles of perseverance and patience – not *once* doubting that you'd make it – and, sure enough, all this effort has paid off, and here you are, sales manager. Great stuff! You have achieved a major goal, and it is not hard to see how happy you are to have reached it. Your smile is a mile wide. I am *extremely* pleased for you, and mighty proud of you, too!

In truth, I cannot remember when I first became a boss. I didn't feel much like one when I started in business because there were only two of us, one of whom was me, and the other didn't need much "bossing." After that, the number of employees grew, and although I cannot pinpoint exactly when it happened, what I will never forget is my realization one day that there were a whole bunch of people who were not only looking to me for direction, but also counting on me for the paychecks that provided their livelihoods. I felt it as an awesome responsibility – which, of course, it was and always will be – but it was nonetheless wonderful and thrilling. Mind you, being a boss did not come easily to me, for in those days (although you might find this a little hard to believe), I felt quite shy and awkward about telling people what to do. There was no one around to give me a few pointers, so I had to learn all the rules by myself, and I know that on several occasions I was clumsy in my dealings with other people. It took a lot of learning, practice, and experience before I developed enough self-confidence to feel comfortable in my role. But, since I am around for *you*, perhaps some of what I learned will be of benefit to you in your new role.

I have always had trouble with the word "boss." One dictionary defines the noun as: master, person in authority, overseer. Person in authority or overseer, okay. But *master*? The days of "we and they" went out with lots of other similar garbage years ago. Needless to say, under no circumstances is it justifiable to make anyone feel on a lower end of the human scale than yourself. Before issuing any directives, the best bosses always ask themselves, "If I were taking these orders from a boss, how would I want to be dealt with here?" It is but a matter of common sense to treat others as you would want to be treated. But then, as Voltaire pointed out, "Common sense is not so common," and as Ralph Waldo Emerson observed, "Nothing astonishes men so much as common sense and plain dealing." Still, whether running a department or an entire company, these qualities are what you must foster and learn to practise well if you are to become a successful administrator.

In place of any archaic notions of "we and they" you must always think of yourself as part of a team. The comparison has been used over and over again, but it is worth repeating. Think of a football team. Yes, the quarterback (the "boss") always gets the ball, and it is up to him to decide to whom it should be given next. Then it is up to that person to run with it, but if his team mates don't help clear his way, he sure as hell isn't going to get very far.

As head of your department, it is up to you to create synergy –the *combined* effect of effort that exceeds the sum of individual effort. Otherwise, you might have one person going off in one direction and wasting a lot of other people's time, or everybody going off in different directions and wasting everyone's time. It goes without saying that you will get much more done if you get a lot of people all going in the same direction. That is what your job is all about. But remember that, just as in football, your team will only be as good as its weakest member.

That is where the importance of communication enters the picture. Since you have delegated them, obviously, you know the responsibilities of each of the members of your group. But as team captain, you must make sure that all members of your group are well informed of each other's jurisdictions, and why and how their combined efforts will bring about the best results. Never forget that only things need management; your people need your leadership.

A leader sets the atmosphere, the standards, and the level of productivity of her group. To do so most effectively, she must first gain the trust and respect of her co-workers, not only through her greater expertise, but also through her constant honesty and sense of fair play, and by always keeping her word. Also, each employee must feel that she has his best interests at heart, that he can always ask for her special help or advice and receive it, and – above all else – that his contribution is being valued and esteemed. Mutual respect is vital. That way, she does not need to issue directives twice before they are met, nor does she have to be the one reported to every time the coffee machine breaks down.

Never, ever, intentionally or otherwise, fail to hear the "heartbeat" of the people you work with. If unrest and dissension spread among your employees, a lessening of efficiency will inevitably follow. Make no mistake about it, there would be no one else to blame but yourself for not having spotted the warning signals in time. Always maintain an "open door" policy. Listen, care, *hear* what your people have to say. Solicit their suggestions, and if some are used, make sure that the contributors are given full and open credit for them at your group sessions. Not only does it do wonders for their morale, it inspires the rest to start thinking how they, also, can help improve productivity. Pretty soon, you will have a lot of free advice that might very well improve your sales department's figures significantly. And that would certainly be a great boost to *your* morale – and to mine, too!

A duty of your new position, which you will probably not like very much but which must sometimes be performed, is that of doling out criticism when it is warranted. Before you do, try to heed William James's advice: "The art of being wise is the art of knowing what to overlook."

I have met people with some pretty unconventional habits which, surprisingly, do not the least impair their work. A salesman who works for a friend of mine, just can't get going in the mornings, when everyone else does. He never makes a call before 11:00 A.M., and yet he is the best salesman my friend ever had. *Results count.* Take it into consideration whenever criticism appears to be in order.

Every now and then, though, you will come across an honest-to-goodness "bad apple"; an out-and-out laggard, chronic complainer, or troublemaker. Be quick to pluck him out of the barrel, for all it often takes is but one person such as this to infest an entire sales force. For this reason, I highly recommend you take the time to check out references very carefully before hiring anyone.

As the new sales manager, you will be under close scrutiny of your staff until you prove your mettle and win their confidence. And if you but wipe that ear-to-ear, Cheshire Cat grin from your face after our celebration dinner tonight, I know you will do just great.

Love,

Your Boss

18 Insurance: The

Great Protector

My Dear Daughter:

I know that your heart stopped as mine did at the sight of the row of red fire trucks at our plant when we returned from lunch on Tuesday. (Nothing jolts one more than a fire truck or a police car at the door!) Fortunately for us, as the fire was confined to our electrical panel, the damage was minimal. I hate to think what it might have been like had the fire occurred after midnight, when no one was in the plant.

Were we insured? That was your first question once our heartbeats had regained normality. As I was answering you that we were, it occurred to me that I had neglected an important part of your management training by not having involved you more in my meetings on insurance matters. It is a subject that usually comes up only once a year, at renewal time, and forgotten about until the next year or when calamity strikes. There are two areas of insurance with which you must concern yourself. One is personal and the other is corporate.

When our friend Doug White died in a car accident recently,

the tragedy was compounded by the fact that there was no life insurance to help his wife and the two very young children he left behind. Doug felt that all insurance agents were "hucksters," his wife told me. Maybe so, but hucksters or not, it still would have eased his family's financial crisis now if he had dealt with an agent and bought some life insurance protection. Left without any money, his wife must now find a job on which she can support her two children and herself, with a great portion of her paycheck going out first to a babysitter. Those are tough straits to be left in.

I started you and your brother off as policyholders at the age of eighteen for the simple reason that I wanted to "insure your insurability." That means that I bought insurance while you were in good health just in case some illness of the future prevented your passing the insurance company's required medical. Once a policy has been issued, it cannot be rescinded regardless of any change of medical status after the date of its issuance. I highly recommend that you and your husband follow the same course for your children.

My insurance agent knows me well. He only quotes me on "term" insurance. That means that I pay a set premium for a period of five years with the option of renewing the coverage at a higher premium rate over each next five-year period. This method is of particular advantage to young people since it allows one the opportunity of increasing coverage as a career progresses and higher wages are earned.

There is no separate investment plan tied to this type of insurance. In my case, I prefer to invest my own money in my own ways rather than have an insurance company invest it for me. Just give me the maximum amount of life insurance *now* for my dollar, in the event that it is needed. And I purchase only two adjuncts. One is double indemnity, which grants payment of double the base policy amount if the holder is accidentally killed (and there is a high incidence of accidental death among young people). The other is a premium waver for disability. This usually provides that should the policyholder become disabled for any reason and unable to pay premiums, he would be covered up to age sixty-five by the insurance company.

When you and your brother were little, I felt good knowing that my life insurance policy would provide ample income for your mother to raise you on should anything happen to me. That was its first major purpose. But it had a second use. I had increased the policy amount over the years, and by the time you and your brother were older and no longer entirely dependent on its proceeds, should I die, it had become valuable collateral against my bank borrowings for company purposes.

There are other excellent uses of life insurance, of course. For instance, it is quite common when a person takes out a house mortgage for the lender to obtain a life insurance policy on the life of the borrower in the amount of the mortgage. This ensures that should the borrower die before the mortgage is paid off, the remainder owing to the lender would be paid to him by the proceeds of the insurance policy. Hence the family is left with a mortgage-free home.

Now let's talk about some other important types of insurance coverage. You will recall that when you and your husband took out the mortgage on your house a proviso of the deal was that you had to have it adequately insured against fire. If fire should destroy it, the insurance company will pay the lender his outstanding loan on your home, and you will receive the balance; and start over. But at least you will have something to start over with! Many people have worked all their lives to pay for their homes and then, because of failing to insure them or not insuring them to a proper amount, have literally watched their life's investment go up in smoke. That is agony!

In addition to house insurance against fire, your insurance agent (note that I do not refer to them as "hucksters") will probably recommend that you also insure the contents of your home against fire, theft, and malicious damage. Take his advice and tell him that you want, as well, the special clause covering such specific expensive items as sterling silver, jewelry, furs, and stereo or video equipment. Most policies today include coverage on house and contents against damage by floods, tornadoes, lighting, and other "acts of God."

Is that all? Not yet. What happens if someone slips on a wet spot in or around your house and falls and breaks a leg or a hip? Or what if you clip someone with a golf ball that hooks off the fairway? The answer is that you could be sued for a substantial amount of compensatory money by the injured party. On the chance that such an accident might occur, you need general liability insurance which, you will be glad to hear, is relatively inexpensive to purchase.

Now are you all through buying insurance? Not by a long shot! Cars, boats, motorcycles, trailers, all need insuring against the damages that might happen to any such possessions or their owners, or to others. Make sure that you buy *large* personal liability coverage as part of this package so that even if you happened to kill or injure a carload of people (heaven forbid), you would have only your remorse (or your conscience) to have to deal with while the insurance company handled the claims of the families of the deceased. Couldn't happen to you? Yes, it could. I will admit that the odds are long against such an accident happening, but I can tell you that I sleep well at nights knowing that should any catastrophe occur, the financial aspects would be the insurance company's concern, not mine.

Just as do many home owners so, too, do many business owners make the mistake of under-insuring or not insuring at all their corporate assets. Machinery and equipment, inventory, office furniture and fixtures, as well as your buildings should all be covered. And make sure that you are adequately insured for the *replacement* value of many such assets, not for what you originally paid for them. In these days of inflation, a building that cost you $250,000 to build ten years ago might very well cost $1,000,000 to construct today. Therefore, you should insure that building for $1,000,000, and not for the $250,000 that it originally cost you.

It is also a good investment for a company to insure the life of the owner and of its chief executives. Very often, a dip in company profits occurs following the death of a senior administrator and, in such instances, the insurance proceeds help the company to bridge the period of time it takes to locate and train a suitable successor.

Product liability coverage is, of course, an absolute essential. If a product or service of yours harms anyone or anyone's possessions in any way (including a product or service of another company), you can expect to be sued for the damage and all that that might encompass. Major dollars have changed hands in court settlements in these cases, and I can tell you that customers and courts are usually not very lenient with the makers of any defective goods or service, especially in cases involving personal injury. Scary business, without an insurance company there to hold your hand!

Depending on the type of business one runs, there are numerous other items that might require insurance coverage, such as autos and trucks owned by the company or non-owned autos and trucks driven on company business, goods in transit, customers' goods on the premises, tenant's liability if you are a tenant, and so on. If a very special type of insurance protection is needed, you might have to turn to the pinnacle of the insurance industry, which is Lloyd's of London. Over the years, they have insured a showgirl's legs, ships in war zones, astronomically expensive jewels, and even against it raining on the day of a major outdoor event. The list of unusual things they have insured make fun reading, but I can imagine that the premiums in some of those cases are anything but funny to the purchasers.

A very worthwhile coverage which, in my opinion, too many companies ignore is against business interruption. Suppose our fire the other day had destroyed our plant. We would have received the funds for the assets we had lost; no problem there. But there would have been a discontinuance of income while our plant was being rebuilt. A business interruption policy pays such fixed costs as bank interest, rent, taxes, salaries (so key people can be kept on until the operation gets going again), and even the extra cost for the auditors to verify the company's losses to the insurance company. Generally, under this clause, I include an amount that would be a straight loss to me if a claim had to be filed. Called a "deductible," it is a small amount, which I feel I can afford to lose but which I save in the lowered premium I pay. The benefit to the insurance company is that it eliminates small claims.

Should you obtain several companies' quotes on your premiums? You should, indeed, but make sure you read all the fine print carefully for, too often, the lower quote usually means lower coverage, not money saved. Insurance companies live in the same competitive world as we do, abiding by the same rules of the game. Yes, you have to pay for what you get, but if you get adequate coverage, you will also never have to worry about being yanked out of business by any hell-or-high-water crisis.

How often have you heard someone say, "I thought it would never happen to me!" Those "its" do occur in everyone's life, both business and personal. My sincerest counsel to you is that you protect yourself *beforehand* against any which might befall you. It sure is one way of making sure you and your family never go broke!

Love,

Dad

19 Women in Business

My Angered Daughter:

Over the years, you have probably fielded most of the hackneyed and commonly overworked male put-downs of the business world: that of being called "Honey" or "Sweetheart" on the job, the "friendly" hugs or "playful" pats on the behind, the more overt sexual advances, and the tacky jokes or needling pokes at your person or gender garbed in the guise of innocently intended humour. You have also faced discrimination in job alignments, in promotions, and in equal pay for equal work performance. All these tribulations you have encountered, we have discussed, and you have overcome in winning and admirable fashion. I admit there were times we had to dig out your Grandmother's tough words, "Don't let the bastards beat you!" to get you back into the fray – but back in you went every time, I am proud to say, with lots of renewed courage and spunk to win your day.

I will never forget how hard I laughed over how *well* you won some of those days. The fellow who persisted in calling you "Sweetheart" around the office and even in front of your clients soon stopped when you changed *his* name to "Cupcake." Patted on the behind another time by one of your bosses, you patted his in return – only with a whalloping good hard swat, to the applause of all the other women in the office. (What a comeback!) Several occasions were most unfunny, of course, such as having to report to the president the serious sexual propositionings of one salesman, and challenging the pay hike far above yours of another because, as you were given to understand, he had a family to support and therefore more expenses to cover than you had as a single person. I have been delighted to watch you follow the advice I offered when you started in your first job.

Now, having overcome all these and many other such harassments and inequities, and after having striven all these years to reach that mighty appointment to the management committee of your company, you want to quit. You want out. You had expected far better of the male gender in the higher echelons of business; far fewer petty prejudices to have to contend with and, instead, there are more – only in different and more subtle disguises than ever before. The other (all male) members of the committee are politely managing to exclude you from major decision-making, the group hasn't yet found sufficient time for a fair hearing or review of any of your proposals and, every time you have tried to press an idea forward, you hear yourself being referred to behind your back as "the pushy bitch."

Well, when has anyone ever promised you that business would become a rose garden at some point? Any senior female executive would be quick to tell you that discrimination against women doesn't just magically vanish at the highest levels of business, and that it probably will not as long as the bulk of the corporate world is run by men, as it is at the moment. You are but a recent immigrant to this kingdom of men, and while you will be welcomed to it by some (the brighter ones), you will be resented, rejected, and fought against more fiercely by many others – perhaps for a very long time to come.

But, you have already stated that you have had it up to the eyeballs with male chauvinism and that you do not intend to put up with it any longer. I cannot blame you for being fed up with it; I cannot prevent you from walking away from it at this juncture or, for that matter, at any juncture of your business or personal life. But I can ask you to reconsider the following before you do so.

As a woman working in the outside work force, you are part of a major, vibrantly alive revolution which started only in this century. As a result of it, women have advanced their status in society more profoundly in recent decades than in any other period in over seven or eight thousand years of recorded history.

Prior to 1900, women worked outside the home only if their income was required to keep body and soul together. Working women were considered lower class and they were looked down upon by the so-called elite – many of whom had little to feel superior about. The unrestricted right to vote for women was only granted by that great arsenal of democracy, Great Britain, in 1928. In the 1950s, it was most rare to be stopped by a policewoman, preached to by a woman minister, defended in court by a woman lawyer, attended to by a woman doctor, or to vote for a woman politician, or – heavens above – to work for a woman boss. None are uncommon events any longer, but consider that it has become so only during your lifetime; that betterments of such enormous proportions for your sex have transpired only since you were born – and that you have actively contributed to their happening! Tell me, as tough as the going might be at the moment, can you really give up and side-step this turning point in history? I think not. I sincerely hope not, for the efforts of your sisterhood have brought about a magnificent increase of the brain power at work in our society, which has contributed vastly to our improved standard of living.

Then why is there still all this small-mindedness and resentment from the opposite sex? I cannot tell you exactly why.

Rampant male chauvinism has subsided to a large degree, but its deep-rooted symptoms still continue to flourish. Witness your mother's experiences over the past three years in trying to bring her mobility aids for the elderly to market. Her biggest problem was getting her male audiences in the manufacturing sectors to produce to her specifications. As thoroughly as she had researched, tested, and proved her designs, countless times they were altered by men who presumed they knew better than she what those designs should be.

Underestimating a woman's intelligence and ability is a failing of many men and because of it many a woman's good and profitable ideas never see the light of day. And when she persists and insists they be given a fair hearing, very often, as you were, she is labelled pushy, militant, or a lot worse. Her male counterpart, on the other hand, pressing an idea forward in identical manner, is termed keen, persevering, a bright young thinker, and all sorts of other complimentary things by his colleagues. Fair? Not at all! Costly? You bet! All thwarted or mishandled new ideas are a waste of company resources. Again, *why* does it happen? I cannot account for the narrowness of many of my gender's minds; I can only hope that it is but a human reaction to the rapid changes in the composition of the work force, and that it is one which time itself will also soon help to correct.

As a worker and executive, you have been a tower of strength in your company for both your male and female employees over the years, but your own gender would suffer most should you walk away from your position now. From what you have said, it would leave no one in the higher ranks of your firm to struggle for equality. A major opportunity blown; a major defeat not only for you, but for every woman in your company's employ. Personally, I would rather see you leave this post for *any* other reason than because of defeat by prejudice. Think about that.

If you decide to stay, I would like to suggest that you try to shed all anger and resentment (as justifiable as it is), and return to this challenge with a "strictly business" attitude. By that I mean that you should view it as you would any other *business* challenge that crosses your desk, such as developing a new product line, charting a new marketing strategy, or retaining a disgruntled customer. Then, leaving all emotion aside, go back into that boardroom and, *by example*, teach the other members of the committee how to become top notch executives, too!

You will do so by remaining unruffled by any attempt to bar your input, or to freeze out your ideas; you will do so by perseveringly presenting your well-thought-out plans and opinions until they *are* given fair hearing and fair evaluation; and you will do so by, at all times, retaining your composure, your dignity, your own unbiasedness, and that extra bonus of yours – your wonderful sense of humour. (Humour is often the best ice breaker of all during many a tense situation.)

By your own impeccable executive behaviour, you will soon reach those of the same true mettle in your group and, while it might take a little longer, I assure you that even the most confirmed chauvinists will follow suit thereafter. Professionalism coupled with perseverance will always win out.

In time, as your position strengthens, you will be able to prevent the stifling of other women in your company by nipping any attempts in the bud. There will always be some dudheads out there who believe that only men can run this world. If our company is to prosper most, you will need to weed them out of your ranks and replace them with brighter minds (of either sex), undiseased by prejudice.

Also, as your position strengthens, you might be tempted at times to want to dish out to men some of the same flack that you have been putting up with all these years. I would ask you to resist such temptations. I dislike female chauvinism just as much as I do male chauvinism, for *both* cost all businesses a tremendous loss of time, efficiency, and profit.

Reflecting on how far you have come in this *male*strom, I want you to know how delighted I am with your progress. Little did I expect to see such a march on business as has been conducted by women over these past number of years, let alone see you among its leaders.

I would have bet the house, my dog, and my airplane only twenty years ago that I would never live long enough to see a woman in the position of prime minister of Great Britain. Hell, not only did Mrs Thatcher get there, she proved herself to be one of the better PMs that great country has ever had. Now if I live long enough to see a woman on the papal throne, I will have witnessed the eighth wonder of the world.

I must go now, for I need to get the shopping done and pick up the dry cleaning before your mother gets home from work – else there will be hell to pay with *my* "boss." (I didn't think I'd live long enough to see that, either!)

Love,

A Member of the Opposite Sex

20 One Day
at a Time

My Dear Daughter:

By the sag of your shoulders these days, no one could doubt the heavy weight they are carrying, and the absence of that ready smile of yours is most noticeable.

From what you told me yesterday, it seems that of the peaks and valleys of business we are seeing a lot more valleys than peaks these days: loss of key personnel, trouble collecting money from a major account, and a weak order book for the next quarter. Indeed, it certainly does seem to be enough to cause the most seasoned of executive's shoulders to droop a little. Or maybe not. Read on.

It is a fact of life that fate bestows more grief and agony upon some people than upon others, as well as upon some businesses more than upon others. Why, no one knows. You can call life unfair, as you have, and you can wallow in self pity, or you can straighten your back and meet both your personal and business problems face on, knowing *you*, not they, are and ever will be in command. When a path becomes strewn with problems, it takes a brave mind to face the difficulties and a thinking mind to work out a plan of recovery. You had better foster both, for your only alternative is to feel as you do now: whipped, woeful, and wretched.

You will, I hope, recall a previous letter to you in which I stressed the imperative of conditioning your mind with positive input if you are to attain positive results. That might seem to be a most difficult thing to do at the moment, but I can tell you that if you are going to win the day, you must first resolve to fight. So let's make a concerted effort at repairing your self confidence – this very moment – with megadoses of that famous medicine called "I Am Going To Win."

There have been times in my life when I have not wanted to get out of bed in the morning and face the world. You might have already noticed that immediately upon awakening, the mind has a pesky habit of passing in review all the potentially tough segments of the day ahead. It is crucial, at that very moment, that the explicit message imparted to your mind be: "I am in control. I am solving every challenge. I am winning." Before I learned how important it is to combat these early bird doldrums, I felt as if my only choice was either cooking in the proverbial boiling cauldron or jumping into the fire. It was not the best way to start a good, productive day, I can tell you.

The key to these tough days is to step back a pace from your long-range company and/or personal goals and assess them on the basis of a shorter time span. This is called *living one day at a time*. The principle of this approach in times of crises is simply to cast the mind into getting you through that–not a week, not a month or a year, but only through one twenty-four hour period. When you wake up in the morning, that's all you can really count on, anyway; none of us can set one foot back into the past nor one step forward into the future, so never concern yourself with either so much that you overlook today. Do not worry now about what your banker is going to say two weeks hence if you do not collect your large customer's account; the crux of the problem is not the banker down the road, but figuring out an arrangement whereby your customer can pay the money owed to you in the meantime. You know it is a solvent company, therefore, there must be a reason for the delay. Get together *today* and work it out. (Undoubtedly, your customer will feel better about it all, and Lord knows, you will, too.) Your other problems must also, of course, be approached in like manner.

At times like this, a little humour goes a long way. In my younger days in business, I had an older man by the name of John Spence in my employ as office manager. John was in his seventies, but always first in in the mornings, always "up," and always there for me. (How I still miss him!) I remember being up to my knees in alligators one day (One day? Many days!) and going to talk to John, looking for some solace. After I had told him all my troubles, his only comment was, "Well, King, things go like that sometimes, and then they get worse!" We had a lot of laughs together over the ensuing years recalling that profound statement of his – it was so accurate: things really never are so bad that they could not be worse.

During my tough times, John would suggest I go into my office, close the door, and for a moment or so concentrate on all the things that were going right in my life – such "trivial" matters, he would say, as great health, great family, comfortable house, good food, terrific friends, and all of them enjoyed in a wonderful and free country. He was so right, of course. These are but a few of the many real treasures of life and they are often those which are the least appreciated, until they are gone. Spence's exercise is one well worth remembering.

Going along with the "one day at a time" approach to problem solving, I wish to draw to your attention that it will require *patience* for it to work effectively. Forbearance is not an easy trait to harness, most especially during younger years, but it is a vital one to include in your bastion against any of life's battles. François Rabelais's long ago comment on the topic was: "He that has patience may compass anything." Shakespeare left behind this observation: "How poor are they that have not patience."

I know you feel you are stuck in a quagmire at the moment, with alligators nipping at your knees as they so often have (and still try to do) at mine. They are no more than a bunch of challenges, all heaped together in one pile, needing your patience to sort, appraise, and solve *one at a time*. Learn to ride out your storms, wave by wave, day by day. As with most else in life, there is nothing new about this system, and it is one that many people use in times of serious difficulties. What they have learned, however, and what I am trying so hard to impart to you, is that this method will only work for those who, while under heavy stress, can maintain the *patience* it takes for clarity of thought to prevail.

Plautus, who lived around 200 B.C., probably facing his own plethora of problems one day, stated, "Patience is the best remedy for every trouble." You will learn, I hope, to practise faithfully his sage advice, addressing your own trials "one day at a time" whenever necessary. (Remember that, as Mr Spence said, "Things go like that sometimes . . . !")

Love,

Daddy

21 Ethics in Business

Dear Julie:

You have been stewing all week over the "deal" offered you by the senior executive of that large company you have been trying to sell to for over a year now. Well, allow me to step in and clear the air for you by Monday. Forget the deal. Drop it like a hot potato! His offer to get you the contract, provided you pay him cash on the side for arranging it, smells to high heaven, and you must have nothing to do with it.

I know that you have gone through all the proper channels within his company and have obtained everyone's required authorization except his. I know the hard work and long hours you have put in trying to land this account and, having come this far, that you might be very tempted to slip a few dollars under the table to this guy in order to finally sew up the contract. But if you did, you would be courting more trouble than I care to think about.

First and foremost, you would be helping this scum to steal from his own company. If we can afford to make such a payment, the money should be used as a saving in the cost to the customer for our goods or service, and not as a neat wad of side money in this executive's pocket. His job is to get the best possible goods or service from his suppliers at the best possible price to his firm. Quite obviously, he is not doing so and, equally obviously, he is a cheat, a liar, and a crook. By aiding and abetting such a person, you, in turn, would become a cheat, a liar, and a crook. Would you like to become one? Then quit entertaining any further thought of this guy's proposal and get on with making an honest buck somewhere else.

This is your first encounter with a flagrant display of dishonesty in business. I am sorry to have to tell you that it will probably not be your last. While most business owners and executives build their companies and their profits by honest and forthright means, there are some who do not; those for whom the motto is "wealth before honour" instead of the other way around. But the business world is too small a place for the unscrupulous to hide for long, and you must not risk tainting your own good reputation by dealing with anyone of that ilk.

During a discussion with a friend recently, I was asked which one of all the letters I wrote to your brother would I leave for him, if I had but one to leave. Without hesitation, my answer was that it would be the one on integrity. In that, I stated, "Owning integrity is owning a way of life that is strong in moral principles – characteristics such as sincerity, honesty, and straightforwardness in your daily living patterns. In the business world, ownership of such characteristics is the lifeblood of any long term success." Please note that I did not say that it was a bonus, nor even one of the most valuable of assets one might possess, but that it is the *lifeblood*–the very "breath of life" – of long-range business success. Yes, a considerable number of people do not employ integrity in their business dealings (let alone consider it the most essential of all traits to own) and, yes, many of them do seem to get away with a lot of dishonesty. But you will find, as I have, that most of them do not get away with it for long. Nothing spreads faster throughout the business community than word of someone's deceitful or unethical practices, and once that word is out, their declining sales usually tell the rest of the story.

Just as charity should, dishonesty, too, usually "starts at home," for who but the parent gets the first crack at shaping a child's character? Unfortunately, as well-meaning as most parents are, it appears that many parents nowadays lean a lot more heavily on the "do as I say" policy of child rearing than on the "do as I do." If a picture is worth a thousand words, an action – the *example* set by a parent – is worth ten thousand more. There's no use telling your kid to be honest while you demonstrate a host of ways of being deceitful, down to chuckling with glee over a mistake in your favour on a restaurant bill, or to beating the speed limit with the aid of the trusty fuzzbuster installed in your car. Unthinkingly and unintentionally, by examples of their own behaviour, many parents teach their children to lie and to cheat, in small ways when they are young, which often lead to much bigger ways when they are older. (Please note that neither your mother nor I have ever chuckled over a mistake in a bill or owned a fuzzbuster. We expect your ethics to follow suit.)

Teachers, coaches, and peers all have a strong influence on the moral growth of each one of us during our school years. In industry, the business leaders take over next. Those who fall short of honest character themselves or who promote anything less than ethical interchange within their departments or companies are those an employee must watch out for most, especially an employee new to the business world, whose own finer instincts have not been corroded by the tacky ways of others. Any employee of an unethical company must get out of such environs and link himself up with a principled cadre in another company. If he does not, he might soon find himself believing, as do a lot of the other people around him, that a little skullduggery, connivance, and backstabbing are all essentials of the corporate game, that everyone plays it the same way or, worse, that he *must* if he wants to become a top notch executive.

Parents, teachers, community and business leaders notwith-standing, the ultimate choice between honesty and deceitful-ness rests with the individual. And if I were not confident to the core of my soul of your choice, I assure you that you would not be occupying the position you are, in one of our leading companies.

A while back you were advised by one of your suppliers that he had to change his quoted price on a chemical because the market price had recently increased. I remember being in your office when you told him to either honour his quoted price or erase your company's name from his client list. That is the stuff of *fine* leadership; the *only* kind our companies need if they are to prosper.

Over the years, it has been my personal credo and my firmest edict to our executives that we maintain the trust of our customers, our employees, our suppliers (and, needless to say, of my bank manager). That policy is the foundation upon which our companies were built and upon which they stand today. We have worked long and hard for our reputation and I am personally very proud of it. As an executive, it is one of your chief responsibilities to make sure that it remains unblemished, for a good name is an invaluable commodity. In protecting it, I hope that you will always find, as I have, that there is a natural high to meeting your business challenges in the honest manner of out-thinking the other guy, not "out-stealing" him. Always remember that it is your integrity and that of all of those who work under you that will keep your company strong and retain its sparkling reputation for honest business practices.

"Truth is the cry of all, but the game of the few," observed George Berkley around 1744. While it might very well be the sport of a select few, it is still the only league to which I wish to belong and I trust that it is so with you. The respect of the busi-ness community is something no fraud artist will ever make enough money to buy or ever savour the pleasure of owning. So let the crooks make their money their way, courting a knock at the door any night by the police, while you and I continue earning ours, our way.

Tell your conniving executive friend that you do not do business his way but that you do have the best product, at the best price, with the best service in town, and that you deserve to be a supplier to his company. Who knows, he might discover that he has a conscience after all, and authorize your contract with no strings whatsoever attached to it. And if you can pull that off, I will buy you the best champagne dinner in the city – for *that* kind of "pay-off," I do, heartily, endorse!

Love,

Your Co-Straight-Shooter

22 The Value
of Creativity

Dear Julie:

What are we going to do about one of our products being whalloped in the market place lately by our competitor's "newer, better, faster" brand? As part of my answer, and because it has enormous bearing on the rest of it later, I first need to make you keenly aware of the environment into which you were born and in which we all live today. We are living through a period of the swiftest change that this world has ever experienced. The statistics are mind boggling. Consider these:

All the information; the sum total of all the information in the world at the time of 1 A.D., the heyday of the Romans, doubled by 1750. By 1900, a mere 150 years later, *this* amount of information doubled. By 1950, only *fifty* years later, the quantity of information in existence in 1900 doubled. By 1965, now only *fifteen* years later, it doubled again. Then, only *eight* years later, by 1973, it had doubled yet again.

Today, it is said to be doubling every three to four years! Think of the enormous volume of information that represents, doubling at break-neck speed during our present times. Does it not stagger the imagination? And it is imagination that is the very thing responsible for this exponential growth. From the imagination – the creative resources of the human mind – have come all the space modules, fax machines, semiconductors, television, lasers, cellular telephones, and thousands upon thousands of other wondrous inventions, all within recent decades. Why now, when our imaginations are no more creative than those of the Romans and of the Egyptians of long ago? The answer is simply that, today, our imaginations can play with an accumulation of knowledge, of science, that is unprecedented in human history – a base to which our forbears greatly contributed, just as we are making our contributions in our turn. As well there has been a greater loosing of the mind's imaginative powers during this century than ever before. Access to education, to knowledge, is more widespread than ever before. And it is expected that the twenty-first century will dwarf the twentieth!

How does all this pertain to our problem at hand, that of countering our competitor's new product? I am sure that you have figured out by now that it has everything to do with the use of creativity, which is an inherent faculty of all human minds. Because a competitor has stolen the march on one of our products at the moment, does not mean we were sitting back, unprepared for it.

Competition forces a company to *think*, and the game revolves around who thinks best, or, in other words, who thinks most creatively. It is essential ammunition for out-thinking or out-planning another's strategy. And creativity is not only imaginative musing, it is also work. It has always been our policy to invest a large proportion of the profits from our manufacturing company in a continuing research and development program. We have recently made several significant breakthroughs in improving our product of the moment, and I feel confident that we will shortly be able successfully to counter the threat being posed by our competitor.

One of my business maxims is that it is prudent *not* to run to the market place with every new improvement, but to store a number of them up for a time such as we are presently experiencing. In short, let your competitor show his hand and, while he is thinking he is getting the upper hand, select the best from your drawer full of innovations and embellishments that will send him reeling back.

In this instance, lesson one for you to remember is this: Many companies pay out a large part of their profits in dividends to shareholders while spending no money at all in developing better or new products. This is a bad mistake. A good company (which I like to think we are) uses its profits by investing a portion in research and development to keep the company alive and kicking for a long time. As our shareholders are all family members, and we have but one banker to impress, our policy of spending today to be in business tomorrow is probably easier for us than it is for others – but I still believe it to be the only route to go.

Lesson two is to realize that for a business to succeed, it is essential to nurture creativity and imagination in the minds of your employees. It used to be that education and willingness to work hard was enough for success to come banging at the door. Not so, not any more. Today's success demands a creative and imaginative mind, as well as knowledge and hard work.

It is a common belief that only a few of us are highly creative and "born" to invent. Certainly, most people do not appear to be innovative or creative. But I believe that creativity is not a conferred power or right of a select few, but innate in all human minds. I think that is exactly what my earlier statistics pertaining to the accelerating accumulation of world information prove.

As a young man starting in business, I was so in awe of my older partner's inventiveness and creative genius that I was convinced I possessed not a smidgen of my own. Happily, time, learning, practice, and experience proved otherwise, but I still wish I knew then what I know now. It would have saved me many periods of unnecessary anguish, upheaval, and uncertainty along the way.

As a little girl, you made the same mistake as I made, and as so many many people of all ages still make. Because you could barely draw stick people in art class or write a poem in English class, you presumed that it meant you were totally unimaginative and devoid of all creative ability. Fortunately, your mother and I had learned enough by then to help you correct that misconception. Creativeness does not manifest itself only in such tangibles as beautiful pictures or lucid and striking prose, or even in great inventions. Originality, inventiveness, and ingenuity evince themselves daily in our lives in hundreds of different ways. While you might not yet even be fully aware of it, your success as a sales executive is largely dependent on the creative thinking you bring to bear on almost all facets of your work, from how best to approach a new client, solve a problem with an existing client, negotiate a contract, bring one to a close, mollify a disgruntled employee, spur your team to greater heights, right down to choosing how best to dress or speak.

Harnessing the creative resources of the mind is a four-pronged exercise. The prongs are: how the mind works; let time pass; solitude; and the master mind. Now let us address each.

HOW THE MIND WORKS: In another letter to you, Mind Before Matter, I explained in layman's terms, my understanding of how the mind works. You will need to reread that letter to implement this program. In brief, all the known facts about any subject you wish to explore must first be stored in your subconscious mind. Then you must expect from your subconscious an unravelling, illumination, or solution of your facts. A series of ideas will come forth, some perhaps at the weirdest of times, but they will emerge and formulate themselves into a pattern for your testing and subsequent action.

LET TIME PASS: It is important for you to understand that each breakthrough of creative knowledge does not happen overnight. Sometimes it does, but generally it takes time–sometimes years – of patient fact-finding and experimentation, and the consignment of all new data to the subconscious while awaiting the final solution. In Robert Frost's words: "How many times it thundered before Franklin took the hint! How many apples fell on Newton's head before he took the hint! Nature is always hinting at us. It hints over and over again. And suddenly we take the hint."

"Taking the hint" from our creative minds has resulted in the wheel, paper, glass, electricity, the car, the airplane; it has put man on the moon, transplanted hearts, provided instant world-wide communication, and all the other magnificent accomplishments of mankind.

SOLITUDE: It is one of the greatest aids to creativity. In order to "take the hint," the mind must have a tranquil environment for the gestation of ideas; a quiet time for new thoughts to surface. As James Russell Lowell opined, "Solitude is as needful to the imagination as society is wholesome for the character." This is why I leave my office on Thursday evenings, not to return until Mondays. Most of my friends think that I take Fridays "off." Little do they know that it is my quiet "thinking" day, which I might spend at home or in a canoe, and the years have proved it to be the most productive and valuable business day of my week.

THE MASTER MIND: In his book, *Think and Grow Rich*, Napoleon Hill defined the master mind as, "coordination of knowledge and effort, in a spirit of harmony, between two or more people, for the attainment of a definite purpose." When two or more people in harmony (which I interpret as meaning tranquility) engage in a "meeting of the minds" to confront a given problem, there is frequently a multiplicity of ideas thrown out for consideration which far exceeds the creativity of each mind thinking independently. It is indeed as if, as suggested by Napoleon Hill, the bringing together of two minds generates the bonus input of an unseen "third" – a master mind.

Creativity and imagination are as inseparable a function of your mind as they are of all those out there advancing our knowledge of computers, the solar system, vaccines, micro-electronics, and space travel. Use it. Trust it. It is the "ammu-nition" I spoke of earlier, and it is of crucial importance within every aspect of both your personal and your business life.

Feed the mind, let time pass for the gestation of ideas in quietness, bring the "master mind" principle into play, and then take your place amongst the greatest inventors the world has known.

What a dreamer I am, you say? Absolutely! Especially on Fridays.

Love

Dreamer

23 Changing Jobs

Dear Employer:

Without question, you will miss Mike Alrest from your sales division. I, too, thought he was excellent and that he would help you lead your sales force to new heights. He will not be an easy member of your staff to replace.

What bothers me more, however, is why you lost such an extremely valuable executive – especially on the heels of another, Cathy Farmer – only two months ago. While the comings and goings of personnel in business is common, the rapid loss of two such key people suggests to me that some constructive examination of their reasons for leaving is in swift order.

Some people change jobs simply for a change of venue, some, as if with ants in their pants, because it is part of their nature never to stay put for long, and many, because searching for some utopian position has become a compulsive habit. These are the drifters who come and go within every company, and they are costly wasters of time and money, for each of their departures means seeking, interviewing, hiring, and training new people to fill their duties. But there are other reasons why people change their jobs, and when they are good performers, losing them is a lot costlier to your company. It takes considerably more training time and practical experience to fill the shoes of a valuable employee than those of a nomad.

As sales manager (indeed, as any executive), you should know all the reasons why employees change their jobs. Only then can you eliminate all the controllable causes from your company and maintain a stable and dependable staff and working atmosphere. If your people know that you are trying your best to enhance their learning, their job environment, and their pay cheques, they will think more than twice before leaving your company.

I believe that not deriving a feeling of satisfaction from a job is one of the chief reasons why people change their jobs – often ahead of money, locale, or dislike of a superior. If there is no feeling of fulfillment at the end of a work day, there is no interest and enthusiasm at the beginning of the next, and no one will put up with that for long. A good boss is on constant alert against the spread of unrest, boredom, and dissatisfaction among her staff. Mind you, the smart employee doesn't leave it all to his boss to provide the satisfaction he wants to feel from his work. He creates a lot of it for himself. For instance, he knows that there is gratification in caring about the company and its future, in looking for and suggesting ways of improving it, in giving his best 100 per cent of the time, and in even such small ways as giving a fellow employee a helping hand now and then. Opportunities and methods of bettering our own circumstances are always there, all around us. Sad to say, they are all too often underrated and unemployed.

Lots of people change jobs because they do not like the boss. Now as much as I, of course, consider you near perfect in all ways, perhaps some of your people do not. Having already written you an entire letter on the topic of being a good boss, I would suggest you reread it just on the chance that you might, indeed, be the sole cause of these recent departures.

Disliking a boss because he is humourless or she keeps an untidy desk is one thing; dislike that stems from a lack of respect for him or her in such areas as fairness, supportiveness, or keeping one's word, is quite another. People will do as little as they can get away with for an employer who is disliked for such reasons, and the best will simply pack up and leave.

Keep your communication pipeline open. Since you are not a mind reader, ask your personnel every several months or so if there are worrisome areas in their work schedules which might need some adjusting or betterment. A lot of good people leave without ever airing their grievances or giving the company a chance to change or improve. They are the saddest cases of all, for both sides lose each time – the employer, and the employee.

One of my now long-term staff members once handed in her resignation because she felt her job was too demanding and that she could not keep up with it. So, before she was fired, she thought she had better quit instead. Fortunately, I had the opportunity of checking into the matter and discovered that she had a totally wrong impression of what her responsibilities entailed – a very far cry from what the company was expecting of her. One relieved person left my office, and one relieved boss saved an employee who is among the cream of our crop today.

Sometimes there is common dislike of a particular individual by the rest of the team members. Checking out why, is well worth your while. If the animosity is based on trivialities, shifting the offending party to another department should be an easy solution to the problem. If the reasons are serious, shift the offender out your front door before you lose good employees because of him. As I have mentioned before, it takes only one bad apple in a barrel to contaminate many of those around it.

Young people in general, and sales people in particular, are usually highly goal oriented and prone to changing jobs if they feel they are not getting anywhere. It is therefore important to review each person's progress on a frequent and regular basis to pinpoint any areas of discontent that can be corrected with a little encouragement from you, or with your personal assistance. Everyone has to feel he is getting somewhere faster than at a snail's pace – and if more than a few of your people are not, your entire sales division will soon be paying for it.

The promotion of a peer or of a friend or acquaintance in another company sends some young people reeling back on their heels. Their immediate reaction is that they are either not as bright, personable, or attractive as the other guy, or that they must be in the wrong job or place not to be doing as well as he. Granted, they could be right on every count, but if they are not, you will need to convince them that skill, knowledge, dedication, effort, and loyalty will always pay off, but in its own time and in due course – not always exactly when they might think it should, or might wish or like.

The lure of higher wages is very often why people leave their jobs for others but, unfortunately, it is not always to greener fields. Many a person makes the mistake of jumping to another company for the extra bucks involved without first having thoroughly explored the conditions of the new position. Frequently, they are disappointing for any one or more of a number of reasons: the company is financially unstable, the boss is a tyrant, the responsibilities are too many or too few, personal growth potential is limited, increased status did not accompany the increased pay, and so on. All such areas of a new position should be delved into *before* and not after an existing one is dropped. Advise anyone who is contemplating leaving your employ to do so thoroughly. Advise them as well to assess their abilities with a level head and to take on neither a lot more nor a lot less than they can handle, for either scenario, sooner or later, usually becomes untenable no matter how much extra salary was initially involved. Upon heeding your counsel, whether your person stays with you or does not, it will still be the best career advice you could have offered him.

Shakespeare wrote, "We know what we are, but know not what we may be." Talk to your people individually and in groups until you have a very good idea of what each would like to be. Only in this way can you be of greatest executive benefit to each, to yourself, and to our company. You will not be able to hang on to all your best staff for all of their working lives, but you will be able to keep most of them if you maintain keen knowledge of their interests, their ambitions, and their welfare. That all starts with what's in their minds. Get it into yours.

In the meantime, I am quitting my job for a couple of weeks of some much desired R & R in my northern woods. I will look forward to meeting Mike Alrest's fine replacement upon my return. (And, I hope, to not many others thereafter!)

Love,

Your Employer

24 Be on Guard

Dear Julie:

Bankruptcy is never pleasant, and I feel very sorry for your friend who is having to close down her business. I know you tried your best to help her, and nothing worked. Indeed, it sounds as if the matter is well past the point of no return.

I also know you have been wondering if the same thing could happen to the company of ours you work for. Well, wonder no longer. It sure as hell could! Just because it's been sailing for years doesn't mean it could not be in trouble tomorrow. Businesses shut down every day of the year. But there are precautionary measures every good company takes to guard against such an occurrence. I doubt your friend had implemented many of them. Make sure you do.

First, though, allow me to stress to you – as you should to your friend – that terminating a business is neither the greatest shame nor the worst thing in the world that could happen to anyone. It is a harsh blow for the owners to have to withstand

(and often a worse one for the creditors), but it does not involve loss of life, only loss of income. A person can recoup from the latter, and not from the former.

Peter F. Drucker, in his book, *Management: Tasks, Responsibilities, Practices*, first made me aware that no business lasts forever. I do not recall his rationale, but from my own business experience, I believe his theory applies for a number of different reasons.

For one, the swiftly paced changes occurring in our society today demand both versatility and the constant vigilance of industry. As the whims of the market place change, you had better be prepared to adapt speedily to what the consumer wants if you want to be around tomorrow. Another, often death-dealing blow to companies comes, of course, when someone else puts out a better product or service than yours. Again, unless you are on your toes and ready to spring into effective counteraction, you might not be counting too many prosperous tomorrows.

But not keeping in step with the shifts of consumer moods, or being unprepared to swing into action against a competitor, are only two of the reasons why businesses go under. There are a host of others, and my guess is that they are far more often the culprits that do a business in than the two causes I have just mentioned. In sum total, they are called *bad management*. There is a lot of it in our world of industry.

Bad management covers a multitude of sins, all of which you must make sure never occupy your premises for long.

First, let's talk about your people. You have often heard me say that in business, you are only as good as the team you have built around you and that that is your primary insurance against corporate failure. But once you have structured your capable group, do not then sit back and give its composition little further attention or monitoring. People change. Most of the members of your group will only get better with time, becoming more adept at their work and more valuable to your team. Chances are, however, that some will falter or fall by the wayside and become a drain on the others because they cannot carry their share of responsibilities. Unfortunately, some of yesterday's top performers do become the "has beens" of today. Personal problems, or too much time squandered at the bar or at the race track, are often the cause. With your eagle eye, you must be able to spot the symptoms before they become serious maladies, and a major problem within your group.

Lack of experience often brings a fine house toppling down. There are so many unexpected curves in industry that many who have spent lifetimes working in it and studying it from all angles, still have difficulty making a dollar. Building a business is hard enough when you have a lot of experience; it is a great deal more hazardous with little or no experience riding on your side.

Expanding a company can be another treacherous affair. Unless you have guaranteed business waiting in line to cover the cost of your expansion and everything that that entails, or unless you have enough money to hold your ground if anticipated business does not materialize on the dot, I recommend against it. I went through a tough experience in this area. One of my major expansions was a touch-and-go affair for a long time before I was able to stabilize it and bring that company into a comfortably profitable position again. (Seems I have bumped up against most of the thorniest problems in business but, happily, I am still here to tell the tale.)

During any, even minor, expansion, the increased costs of larger premises, extra staff, additional equipment, and greater debt will chew away at your savings account very rapidly. If there is imminent danger of your reserve being all gobbled up, you will need to move more rapidly. Your choices then are few. Drumming up enough new business to get your company back to a break-even point is one, and, needless to say, it is the happiest and most preferable of all. Finding an investor who can bring business with him, or one who owns enough of a bank roll to ride out your storm, are two other alternatives. Another is to sell the moveable parts of the business to a competitor and close down your operations. The last, ugliest, and most painful, is shutting down the business outright, with or without a receiver to handle the bankruptcy details which will likely follow shortly thereafter.

Facing these choices is not easy. Your heart will want to stay, while your head keeps insisting you should go, meanwhile there will likely be a banker somewhere, urging you to hurry up and make up your mind because his patience is wearing very thin.

In his book, Peter F. Drucker advises us to stick to the businesses about which we know most. All too frequently, flushed with success in one line of enterprise, many business leaders branch out into faraway fields about which they know nothing, only to flop back very hard on their behinds. Why? Probably only because that important experience factor I mentioned earlier was either vastly underestimated or most grievously overlooked.

There are a number of others reasons why businesses fail all of which fall under the heading of bad management. Among them are poor planning, lack of persistence, procrastination, a backsliding in quality control, a declining level of customer service, late delivery, questionable business ethics, weak pricing policies, and feeble marketing strategy. But there is another reason for the demise of some companies which is an entirely honourable one.

There is no disgrace to wrapping up a business because of circumstances that are truly beyond your control. For instance, picture yourself a manufacturer of buggy whips when the automobile first hit the market. You might not have had any choice but to fold up before you lost the shirt off your back. (But then, knowing you, you probably would have been manufacturing car phones before the automobiles took hold!)

In summation, as long as owning a business is your career,

you will never be free of what I call guard duty. It is an integral function of that select calling, and the only way you get to print on your letterhead, ''Incorporated for over thirty years.''

Love,

Father

25 Starting a Business

My Aspiring Entrepreneur:

For some weeks now you have been attempting to extract some firm opinions from me on the wisdom of starting a business of your own. By now, you might be thinking that my evasive answers to date indicate a lack of interest or enthusiasm on my part. Far from it. As I usually do, I first wanted to absorb every point you had to make and then ponder and weigh each for a while before getting back to you. Having now given them all considerable thought, I felt my impressions and views might best be expressed by letter for your contemplation.

So the "owning my own business" bug has finally bit you, too. I expected it would, sooner or later, because of the certain traits you possess that generally lead one to think in that direction. But thinking about it and successfully doing something about it, as I am sure you already know, are two horses of very different colours.

Most people have three main reasons for wanting to own their own businesses: first, to make money and to savour all that that can bring, particularly being hailed as successful; second, to be their own boss; and third, for the thrill and excitement associated with running their own show. Judging from our conversations, all three enticements seem to be at the top of your want list. Well, I have no argument with your desires for they were mine, too, when I chose the same route for my life's work. It has been very kind to me and, with enough good planning, gumption, and sagacity on your part, it can be kind to you, too. However, it is not a track that has been benevolent to everyone, and for this reason, and because too many people have learned the dangers of ownership the hardest way – through failures – I would like to make the following assertions on the topic.

You want to make a mint load of money and, by so doing, be regarded as successful. Well, prosperous business people are looked upon as symbols of success, all right; there is no doubt about that. But I want you to remember that there are many other successful people out there whose prime objective is not to make money, but to be the best in their field. There are scores of doctors, policemen, dedicated public servants, artists – the list is endless – for whom the quality or value of their work far outranks any monetary grading. Do not neglect to include them in your honour list of role models.

Of course, you have heard the old saying, "Money can't buy happiness." Whenever I heard it said when I was your age, I always wisecracked back, "Oh yeah? Just give me the money, and I'll do my own shopping, thank you very much." Well, now having lived a little longer, and having acquired a few bucks and done a lot of my own shopping, I can tell you that that old saying is gospel. Money cannot buy respect, which is earned, nor love, which is given unconditionally, nor health, which is heavenly bestowed. And that, among the few other things I have learned, is what happiness is really all about.

By wanting to be your own boss, you are manifesting your independent spirit. Being directed by other people (especially if the direction is poor), often becomes demoralizing and, indeed, you might very well be better off and far more productive without it. However, becoming your own boss as a result of owning your own business is not always as clean cut a benefit as many think. In almost every instance there is a banker looming somewhere in the background to whom every boss is answerable to some extent, every hour of the day, every day of the year.

But, bankers aside, let us proceed. We have established that you want to make money and that you want to captain your own ship. Your next decision must be which type of vessel would be best suited to your command. There are hundreds of types of businesses from which to choose, but I would recommend you opt for one in which you have had some experience. Most businesses are run by professionals with years of know-how. Pitting yourself against them as an amateur could be foolhardy. Their advantage, of course, are those years of trial and error during which they gained experience by learning how to survive their mistakes.

Blazing trails is most admirable and I have nothing but respect for the many who, with no experience, only belief, turned their dreams into businesses. But for every such remarkable feat, there are hundreds which go down to defeat. The odds are that you, as most of us, would be most fortunate to survive a new venture without experience in that field–unless you happen to have a ton of money to keep you going during your period of learning. "There is not a fiercer hell than the failure in a great object," wrote John Keats. Since I do not want you to experience that hell, and I know you do not own a ton of money, I sincerely advocate that you evaluate your business experience carefully and the types of business to which it is best suited before and not after you take the big plunge.

If it seems as if I am only stressing a lot of the negatives you might have to encounter along your road to riches instead of trying to imbue you with the confidence and courage it takes to "go for it," that is not the case. My intent is only to illuminate for you some of the problems others have stumbled over in starting businesses, which need not become yours. In this vein, I offer you more food for profitable thought.

You've often heard it said, I am sure, that it takes money to make money. Well, it does, but it is a multiple game. It is not hard to make a million dollars a year if you already have ten million. Any nice safe government bond will give you 10 per cent interest on every dollar you invest. But making more money than that cozy guaranteed 10 per cent on your investment is what is now the issue, your desire, and your challenge. How does one go about doing that at lowest possible risk? For certain, it is a matter of knowing exactly just how much you can afford to invest in a new venture without it presenting any danger of bankrupting you. In other words, invest only what you can afford to lose. This is a very conservative rule of thumb, but one that has a lot of merit. Many a person has turned a small business into a giant business by gradually reinvesting capital in ever larger amounts. But their guiding principle was never to entrap or indulge themselves in anything too costly to absorb if their best laid plans went awry. (And I can personally attest that some sure-fire platforms do go askew; all too often, it seems sometimes.) When those hot new opportunities are too big for one's britches but just too promising to pass by, it is time to bring in some money partners to help share the financial risk. But this seems to be one of the hardest lessons for some business people to learn.

Your next move? Market research. Do not toss serious money behind any new service or product without first preparing a strong market research program. There is a great deal of money squandered away in the business world by so-called executives who fail to conduct proper and incisive analysis of their market prior to entering it. Market studies of advertising techniques, packaging presentations, pricing policies, and testings of consumer reactions to your new service or commodity can usually be accomplished at reasonable cost. Try as best you can this way to prove your methodology and product potential before any major launch else you end up with what we older executives refer to as an "Edsel." That was a new car Ford brought out around 1960 which flopped miserably on the market, creating both financial upset and harsh embarrassment for this world-renowned corporation – and all because of inadequate market research and analysis. It is a classic example of a company not doing its homework carefully enough; not "feeling the pulse" of its consumers and reading correctly their current preferences.

I think you have gathered by now that if you are craving the excitement and adventure of running your own show, there will be plenty of that. You will not see it, but you will be well aware of the roulette wheel constantly whirring behind you on which most of your chips are riding daily. If you have borrowed money as well as invested your own in your new enterprise, the stakes will be even higher; lenders want personal guarantees to ensure that, while they may lose some money if your business fails, you will first lost the shirt/blouse right off your back.

Worrisome? It can be, if you are not built for living on that sharp edge called risk. (Something the socialists never think about when describing how they would like to tax our profits away.) Scary? Awesome? Intimidating? Sure, it is all of those – but that's what makes it all adventurous. If your grandmother were here, she would have one comment to make on our topic, her favorite: "Nothing ventured, nothing gained." I concur, with one proviso: that as you set out, you include some precautionary measure against financial debacle down the road. Some big winners maintain one must gamble all to win. Well, that can remain their strategy; it will never become mine. Steady investment of what I can afford to risk has always been my credo, and I find all the adventure I want – and then some – in that method of building businesses.

I have often talked to you about hard work. Outside of some learned medical doctors I know, there are few others who work as long or as hard as most business owners. Forty hours of labour per week and four or five weeks of holidays a year are not common to this profession – at least not until success has permanently ensconced itself on your doorstep.

Co-ordinating an organization entails blending experience, research, management, time schedules, government inspectors, consumers, bankers, egos, taxes, suppliers, and employees, and moulding them to your policies and procedures. It means living on that "edge" I spoke of earlier all the time, for there will seldom be interludes during which no severe problems are threatening to chew into your profits. The tension goes with the territory. All in all, owning your own business entails a gruelling amount of work and, often, an inordinate amount of pressure. There will be days you might wonder why you ever got yourself into the horserace, for that is exactly what it is like; and just as the horseraces run daily, so must you, and at least the same, if not a much faster pace.

You have always been a hard worker; there has never been any question about that. My only concern would be that you keep a balance between your fervour for making money and your pursuit of happiness, and that you never confuse the two and mistake one for the other. Amassing enough money to be able to buy anything one's heart might desire is wonderfully intoxicating, but it can be a shortlived and shallow happiness if, as you make all your millions, you do not take the time to care for your health, your self-esteem, your family, and your friends. I would not call that being successful.

George Bernard Shaw wrote that: "People are always blaming their circumstances for what they are. I don't believe in circumstances. The people who get on in this world are the people who get up and look for the circumstances they want, and, if they can't find them, make them."

Some people want only quiet circumstances: a quiet job and a quiet existence. You are of a different mettle, desirous of challenge, adventure, risk, and you are full of courage, to boot. Not for you the phrase, "I wonder what would have happened if. . . ." There is every good reason for you to consider starting your own business – creating your own circumstances – and if you are free next Tuesday, I will be delighted to discuss all your ideas at greater length. I must warn you, however, I will not make it easy for you to leave your present position within our companies; your value to us has become immeasurable. But I do promise to keep my personal emotions aside for, as much as I would love you to remain, much more I wish not to restrain or impede either your looking for or making those circumstances Shaw wrote about.

With warmest regards,

"George"

26 Good Advice

Dear Julie:

Our meeting this morning has led me to put pen to paper this evening. Installing an advanced computer program within your company certainly calls for some careful thought and deliberation. Computer installation has driven many a corporate executive to want to contemplate suicide. As simple a matter as we are all led to believe it is, it is not.

I sense your concern over this new move since you have had absolutely no experience with such a venture before. Do not be embarrassed by the fact; most other executives have had no more than you at the same juncture. The big difference is that many forge ahead with their resolutions relying on a few skilled people from the computer installation company to see the project through, instead of seeking some experienced outside counsel beforehand, as is your intent. My compliments on this excellent decision. You are correct that neither you nor any of your staff are knowledgeable enough about computers to undertake this expensive purchase and oversee its implemen-

LETTERS FROM A BUSINESSMAN TO HIS DAUGHTER

tation on your own. You have just saved yourself a load of headaches, frustrations, and lost time.

I know little about the workings of sophisticated computer programs, but I have heard stories from many of my associates about their initial experiences with them that would make the devil himself cry. And in almost every instance I was cautioned to hire a consultant first if I were considering taking the same computer route. So, now we are. And my best advice to you is that we take their advice and hire ourselves a consultant.

What we need is an expert adviser with a proven record in his field who will help us decide the answers to three main questions: who is best to contract for the work? what program should we adopt? and what equipment should we purchase? How do we go about finding such a person? Certainly there are many consultants around, but a lot of them are consulting only because they cannot get regular work. (That might be cruel to state, but it is a fact.) I would think that the business associates I mentioned earlier would be our first best bet at locating a reliable person. I suggest you give them each a call, explain your position, and ask whom they would recommend for the job. I can tell you that every one of these executives has had enough experience in this realm by now to know which consultants are worth their salt.

Meet with each recommended consultant personally and spell out where you think computers would improve the efficiency of your operations. Those who are interested in acting as your counsellor will then offer to prepare an outline for your consideration of how you should proceed with the project under their guidance. At this point, you should ask each for the names of four or five former satisfied customers. The prima donnas among the group will be offended by your request for references, as if it were a personal affront. Pay it no mind. Just cross their names off your list and make your selection from among those who are pleased to comply with your request. You need never apologize for asking anyone for references – and it is a very good practice, always, to verify them.

Once having selected your senior adviser, meetings, meetings, and more meetings will follow as you both go through the process of evaluating computer companies, (checking out *their* references, too, please), and then reviewing their presentations and setting prices and schedules for the completion of the work.

There are many other intricacies of business besides the selection of a computer system that might well warrant seeking outside professional help by a company. During my own career, I have employed consultants to help us solve production efficiency problems, improve internal communications, reconstruct a sales force, overhaul an advertising campaign, assist in labour negotiations, and help in the structuring or restructuring of our financial affairs, because of corporate income tax concerns. You name it, and an experienced specialist can be there to assist you in most corporate matters. It is one of the best ulcer-calming treatments going.

Some executives have too much ego to seek such outside help or, if they do give it serious thought, decide against it because it "costs too much." I compliment you again for having allowed no such deterrent to interfere with your plain good judgement in the matter of computerization. It amazes me how many people plunge themselves and their companies into serious predicaments, which only increase in velocity with time, by believing they can solve every problem or handle any new development on their own. This kind of executive makes me very nervous. But then, on the other hand, so does the type who needs someone else to confirm that two and two still equals four. There is an amount of personal professional knowledge that every good executive must possess or should be able to obtain on his own. Common sense and good judgement should then dictate when a little, or a lot, of outside assistance is sound and economically practical in order to ensure the successful execution of a new policy or the solving of an old problem.

Still other executives, while owning enough smarts to bring in a consultant, lack the brains or the fortitude it might take to implement what is usually the high-priced advice of a consultant. Many excellent reports lie gathering dust in the desk drawers of senior executives, never to see the light of day. I am not suggesting that you accept and act on every suggestion an adviser might make. Far from it. Question, argue, or discuss any area of contention until you are that convinced the recommendations are sound and you are anxious to put them into effect. But right from the beginning, give your counsellor every ounce of information you can that will help him help you. Without it, his job will certainly be a lot tougher and, therefore, take a lot longer to fulfill—at your expense, both in time and in money.

Good consultants evaluate the personality traits of their clients as well as the facts of a situation. They are adept in counselling without a hint of pomposity or showiness, and the best do not feel they have earned their fee until they have satisfactorily pesuaded a client that their proposals should be carried through.

You have undertaken a major program for your company. Good advice can go a long way toward your seeing it up and running on schedule, on budget, and to everyone's benefit, delight, and applause. It will entail your staying in close touch with your consultant daily, making sure there is a free exchange of information, and keeping an open mind to all of his suggestions. Your common sense, of which my own mind tells me you have a lot, should take good care of everything else.

By the way, while there is little I know about hi-tech computer systems, there are some avenues of business about which I have learned quite a bit. My door will always be open to you for consultations in any of these departments. The fee? *You* pay for lunch at one of *my* favorite restaurants for a change.

Love,

Your Adviser

27 Equal Time

Please

My Dear Daughter:

I was sorry to have missed you last Saturday when I dropped by your home, and sorrier still to hear the tone of your husband's voice when he told me that you were spending most Saturdays and many evenings at the office of late. It didn't take genius to grasp the fact that, while he is more than willing to carry his equal share of home and family responsibilities, his share has been anything but equal for a long time now. Item one.

Item two is that the last couple of times you and I had lunch together, you were curt and churlish with our waiters, a direct opposite of your usual courteous and considerate self. It is not my intention to insult your intelligence but, to my way of thinking, neither of these are small matters; indeed, they could be major if they signify that a growing preoccupation with work is causing a growing insensitivity to your other responsibilities in life and to the feelings and needs of the other people in your life.

Speaking not only as your father but as someone who knows the haunting of hindsight, I caution you most sincerely to heed these warning signals. Stand back. Review. Your job has gradually demanded more and more of your time; now it is taking up most of it. Many jobs do that, especially such open-ended ones as yours in sales and marketing. I have always promoted hard work to get ahead, but I have also always preached the importance of a balance in life. Is there balance in yours? Or, engrossed in your work, are you unthinkingly taking regular advantage of those at home—most especially of your husband's support, cooperation, and love? Success, knowledge, and experience are no guarantee against vulnerability, no assurance against falling into the traps we all swear at the outset we will be smart enough to avoid.

I once knew a young policeman who, to everyone's joy at the time, was promoted to the position of detective. Little did he and his wife expect the family hardships and near chaos that his promotion would inflict on their lives. Dedication to the job entailed not only his often having to work around the clock for days, but being called to report on a case at once, no matter whatever else he and his family might be in the middle of doing: dinner, a hockey practice, a school function, a visit with the kids' grandparents, or even a bedtime story.

Promise after promise had to be broken to his two young sons, who did not understand why a commitment to his job always had to take precedence over his time with them. "Depending on Daddy" started to hold little meaning to them. And, in due course, "When is Daddy coming home?" changed to "Doesn't Daddy live here any more?"—and then to not asking about his whereabouts at all. Mindful of the ill effects such parental inconsistency would have on their sons' happiness, the wife pleaded with her husband to change his job within the force to one with more regular working hours. It was to no avail. He felt that he was only doing his best to provide for the family, that it was his wife's responsibility to stand in for him with the boys whenever necessary, and that by so doing, everything would turn out hunky-dory in the end.

The wife disagreed. Believing that a stable one-parent household would be better for her growing children than the uncertainty of the existing one, she told her husband that she was taking the kids and moving out. I am happy to say that she did not and that the story ends on a positive note. Not too many people would knowingly give up their families because of the demands of any occupation. He changed jobs within the department and I know for a fact that peace, cooperation, and stability have reigned in that household ever since.

It is still sad, however, that the entire family had to go through such lengthy turmoil and near crisis before their problem was resolved. When problems arise today, both of these parents now have enough knowledge and experience to know how to handle them better. Do not wait until you are sixty to draw on what *you* have already learned in life. Only by "stopping the music" now and then do we hear a sweeter tune when it starts up again. Stop the music for a while and reflect on what matters most in your life; then consider whether what matters most is being tended best in your life.

Since I have butted in this far (my courage bolstered by my extra thirty years of experience over you on this planet), I might as well go all the way and voice a few further opinions. Your husband has been shuffling his work hours around to accommodate yours for a long time now, and 80 per cent of the time he is the one looking after the kids and the house while you are away at the office. In times of emergency or special circumstances, no good partner resents double duty. It is generally given freely and gladly and expected of one another. It is called sharing, which is really what marriage is all about. But no spouse, no matter how much he or she loves the other, will continue carrying an unfair workload forever. You are in a fog if you think your husband will.

Nothing in life – and this includes spouse, children, work –

should demand all of your time. It is part of human nature that whomever you give 100 per cent to will always want more. There must always be something *left* to give. If you work midnights and Saturdays habitually, you will eventually adopt these hours as standard for your job. Eventually your extra work will become more expected of you than appreciated, and you might find it very hard to rein back without spoiling your image. In the meantime, you will have missed special family times or occasions with friends which cannot be recaptured. If you sacrifice too much, you will find your rewards as satisfying as that extra piece of chocolate cake which, seconds after it's eaten, you can't remember why you had to have it, but the burden of the extra pounds is still there to be paid for.

I suggest you sit down to your most important board of directors meeting ever, one with your husband and your children, and discuss a rebalancing of priorities. I should like to think you will immediately resume your turns for reading bedtime stories to the kids, or picking them up from school, or taking them to the dentist or to their music lessons. I should like to think you will promptly revive your weekly evenings out with your husband and your frequent get-togethers with your friends and the other members of our family.

Freeing up all that time from work is a lot easier said than done, you say?

Granted. But need I ask whether it is worth it?

Love,

Buttinsky

28 Borrowing Money

Dear Borrower:

As our senior marketing executive, you have done great work in defining our reasons for wishing to expand our chemical division. Your market analysis is sound and thorough and your projections are valid and realistic. Congratulations, because without such a sound study no lender would open his vaults to provide us the funds we require for this expansion.

While you were preparing this part of our presentation, I was compiling with others some additional vital information. Lenders speak a special language called "numbers." This is an area of expertise for which a highly qualified accountant really earns his salary, and then some. It was essential for our accountant to translate all the details of our plans into figures–the costs of the manufacturing facilities we will need, the accompanying costs of production, increased overheads, estimated new sales, cost of new sales, cost of advertising, the profits we expect over the next three to five years, the amount of the loan required to support our new venture, the interest costs thereof, and the repayment schedule we propose. Only in this way can the lender readily follow the financial conclusions being presented for his consideration. A separate report includes pertinent information on the owner, on our management team, a synopsis of the company's history, and our current organizational structure.

Over the years, I have had several projects which I knew were right for one or the other of our companies turned down by lenders because of insufficient data in our presentation. On another occasion, a lender readily provided the funds for a venture that was most inadequately thought out. (It failed miserably, by the way, because of our lack of pre-planning. I wished that time that the lender had kept his money and, I am sure, so must have he.) Just recently I was told by one of my lenders that he is astounded by the number of people who come to him as ill prepared as we were that time; full of vim, vigour, and enthusiasm, but not much else. There are cardinal rules of borrowing. Please imbed it in your mind that the first rule is a sound and realistic corporate plan. I believe that our plan is now strong enough we can approach a lender.

Which lender should we approach is the next question. The degree of risk inherent in our plans – as it is in all such ventures – most often determines who is the most likely to consider lending us the bucks we want. There are all sorts of categories of lenders in the financial field. The trick is to select the category best suited to our needs.

In simplified form, there are three main categories of lenders. There are the banks who charge interest on their loans and with whom principal repayments must be met within specified time frames. Generally, the risk involved for the bank is relatively minimal. A second source is often referred to nowadays as *venture capitalists*. Their terms are usually a comparatively high rate of interest *plus* part ownership of your company. Your third option, of course, is to borrow from a private source; from your Uncle Ed, the local doctor, a friend, or another business person, on whatever terms are agreed upon between you. If the commercial lenders have refused to cooperate because of the high degree of risk involved, this might be your only recourse. For people with only a great idea and no assets to speak of, it is probably the only route open to them, and there are many millionaires who started out this way. There are many others, though, who started out the same way and ended up losing their shirts and their lenders', too, in the process.

My experience tells me that we should talk to our banker first. He will try to help us in whatever way he can and his professional assistance is a valuable commodity. If, after careful study of our proposal, he is unable to loan the funds exactly as we have requested, he will likely get back to us with several other methods of borrowing our needed money from his bank. Or, if he cannot accommodate us at all, he will probably recommend a few lenders who will – probably venture capitalists – or he might propose a joint venture between his bank and a venture capitalist or with another type of lender. I must emphasize the importance of allowing sufficient time for any such negotiations to gel. Many people, consciously or subconsciously, make the mistake of pressing their lenders, first, for their immediate time and, secondly, for their conclusions. This is not conducive to obtaining their most valuable input.

There are other mistakes that can be easily avoided as, for instance, in the matter of working one's way into a financial institution. Rather than calling up a lending officer cold and asking for an appointment, supply him first with a good referral. It is guaranteed to warm up the atmosphere considerably for that first meeting with the person whose money you want to spend.

One day recently when I met my banker, he was totally exasperated. Some fool had just taken up two hours of his time on an iffy transaction that should have taken no more than thirty minutes. Name dropping had eaten up most of the time.

Thinking it would impress the banker, this would-be borrower had tossed into their conversation the names of everyone he had ever brushed shoulders with, from the mayor to the prime minister. It did not sew up the deal. Rather, as the banker confided to me, this guy's ship was sunk fifteen minutes after it had left the harbour.

"Freebies"—gifts, or long lunches or dinners—carry about as much weight as name dropping does when it comes to dealing with most lenders of paper gold. Trying to buy your way into the heart of a financial institution's executive is stupid. Loan officers operate according to set guidelines. Asking them to bend or break them is asking for trouble whether you are refused or granted your request. If you are turned down, you have lost forever any creditability you might have had in the first place; if accommodated, you have only hastened the day the executive gets booted out the door, and your account and reputation along with him.

Now let me tell you some of my thoughts about what constitutes a good financial establishment for a businessperson to deal with. First, I like one that is not forever changing its lending managers around. I quit two large banks partly for this reason. I got tired of having to educate a new account manager about my complicated business affairs every twelve months or so. The other half of the reason I left was because it took them an unreasonable length of time—up to eight or ten weeks—to respond to my requests for funds.

Many bankers claim that both these snags are just part and parcel of dealing with a large bureaucratic organization. Maybe so, but I think both are more due to the lack of a decentralized program that would allow approval of large loans by local managers rather than by a single invisible credit manager somewhere out there. Proof of that is the bank that I am with today, which is about the twentieth largest in the world. Its executives have security of geographical tenure which eliminates my having to familiarize someone new with our accounts every year or so and which allows them to respond to my proposals with an, "It's on," "It's off," or "We are looking for alternatives," within about two weeks.

I never met a credit manager, a district manager, or a division manager in the twenty years that I had the other banks' money. My current bank has seen the colour of my eyes through their president, executive vice-president, and credit manager. No more robots to deal with; just damn fine top financial executives who come out of their ivory towers and meet their customers on their home turf. I like to know personally who I am conducting business with; who is making the decisions on my account. I am pleased that they, too, want to know who they are dealing with on a personal as well as on a balance-sheet basis.

A lender negotiates with two words at the forefront of his mind: risk and security. The key to successful borrowing is finding a comfort zone wherein the lender feels his risk in lending you his money is offset to a reasonable degree by the security or the *collateral* you put up against your loan. The more risk there is involved to the lender, the more security you will be asked to provide. I have always been able to borrow what money I have needed mostly perhaps because I have never been shy about putting up adequate security. Many business owners, however, are reluctant or even refuse to provide guarantees against their requested loans. That puts the lender in an almost impossible position to try to negotiate a deal, especially if the integrity of the client is unknown to him or if his track record has yet to be proved.

Our banker will assess the following key areas of our presentation in depth: the purpose of the loan, the talent and record of the management, the current financial position of the company, our future financial ability to pay the interest and capital repayments of the proposed debt, and the level of security being provided.

If he turns us down and wishes not to discuss alternatives or even refer us to other lending institutions, he might well be giving us a major (and our best) piece of advice for free: to go back to the drawing board and review this entire project from top to bottom again.

If he says yes, we will let *him* pay for our next business luncheon. After all, we are the customer.

Financially yours,

Dad

29 Reaching for the Top

Dear Julie:

Seldom have you made a decision over all the years we have shared together that I felt necessitated any interference from me. But, as much as I have always wished not to interfere with your life in my dual role as your father and your employer, I feel compelled to challenge your most recent major decision.

Now that your president has announced his plans to retire in six months, I am at a loss to understand why you have decided against asking to be considered as his replacement. It took Herculean effort to attain your present position of vice-president of marketing–effort that at times placed a lot of strain on your family life, but you and your husband overcame these difficulties exceedingly well. With that aspect of your life in happy order, with your executive skills highly esteemed by all, and with your success so far in climbing every rung of the corporate ladder save the last, why turn away from reaching out for the top rung now?

From our brief conversation about it, I gather there are three main areas of concern to you: the job would entail too much time, too much hassle, and you believe that you are under-qualified for it. The father in me suspects that there might also be a tinge of fear lurking somewhere in the background: a fear of the unknown. Let us dissect that possibility first.

What, exactly, are the unknowns about taking on the presidency of your company? Without doubt, it is another big challenge. But you are well used to those. Nothing new to fear here. To summarize the duties, the position involves applying your skills, albeit on a wider scale, to personnel selections, orga-nizational matters, and profit and loss statements. Anything here that you have not done before? Nothing. Good! I used to remind you often of Thoreau's words, "Nothing is so much to be feared as fear." Perhaps you just need to be reminded of them again. Now let's move on to your three stated reasons for this cessation of your upward momentum.

Too much time being required by the job holds no water with me. It is my observation after thirty-five years in the busi-ness world, that the best presidents are experts at time man-agement. They measure carefully the hours in a day, a week, a month, and in a year and calculate how best they can be utilized to maximize their talents, their needs, and their desires. They are masters at allocating sufficient time to their jobs and to everything else that they enjoy in their lives – family, friends, travel, charitable work, exercise, relaxation, or just plain thinking.

In my opinion, the best of these executives are those who run their businesses four days a week with intensive involve-ment with employees, management, customers, bankers, researchers, government officials, and so on, and reserve the fifth day for thorough review and careful organization of their coming week or month in peace and quiet. It is a thinking day, and thinking is, after all, what a president gets paid for doing best.

Presidents who spend too much time on daily business are probably performing too many duties that, especially if they are repetitive and of a time-consuming nature, should be delegated to someone else. You are already highly skilled in time management, having for many years now most laudably balanced your time between your husband, three young children, your home, your friends, and your career. If you can juggle that as well as you have all this time, I do not see any reason why you could not now include handling the presidency–especially since your youngest child will soon be joining the other two at high school.

Your second determent is that there are too many hassles attached to the job. If there *are* too many in the president's office, it is because the occupant has failed to organize the place properly. Hassles – as well as their antidotes – are created by people. The more good people you select who can take on responsibilities and duties and run with them to the finishing line, the fewer hassles there will be crossing your desk. Time and time again, we have talked about the importance of building business around people, and of teamwork, and synergy. This principle still is and will always be the backbone of good business.

Without doubt, life in the corporate world has a lot of unnecessary problems. For years, you have coped with some stupid accounting policies, weird production problems, and the refusal of the existing president to accept your word that they needed to be rectified. These problems have affected both the morale and the efficiency of your division. Just think, as president, you could correct any such niggling situation whenever one might arise, remembering at all times that only the *real* challenges of running a business – not the petty hassles – are there to test your mettle.

And so to your third point. You think you have too little talent to bring to this exalted position. There is the greatest good in assessing your abilities realistically so that you do not bite off more than you can chew. But *under*estimating your skills in this case would be as great a mistake as overestimating them. Your record, your *experience*, is the base requirement of this

169

position; it is the "arch" upon which to build the vision, leadership, and determination demanded of a fine president.

Vision means deciding where you want your company to go, and by when; good leadership means charting the course and selecting the right people who will help you get it there; determination is what will get you there despite any disruptions that might occur along the way. (If you need to measure your own determination, tally up all the planned projects you have failed to achieve over the past ten years. The list is short, huh?)

Remember that, as Theodore Roosevelt wrote, "Far better it is to dare mighty things, to win glorious triumphs, even though checkered by failure, than to take rank with those poor spirits who neither enjoy much nor suffer much, because they live in the gray twilight that knows not victory nor defeat."

Presidents who fail are very often poor organizers. You are not. They are often tepid communicators. You are not. Frequently, they are weak at finding key people or top consultants. You also are not. But being a president does not mean that you have to know everything (no one does, some only think they do); you just must know how to co-ordinate and keep the various functions of your operation purring along as one, and be quick about pinpointing problem areas and correcting them. Never yield to the theory that, "If it ain't broke, it don't need fixing." Just because you have a good product or service does not mean it could not be made better. If you do not keep looking for ways of improving its quality, its performance, its cost to the company or to the consumer and so on, someone else surely will.

But, all of this you already know, or else the department which you now run would not have excelled as steadily as it has since you first took it over. In my opinion, there would be no trick to your working exactly as you have been for a long time, but from the president's chair now. (It is a little higher than yours, and the leather is a little finer, but I think you could handle that, too!)

I have attached two airline tickets for you and your husband to your favourite spot by the sea. It would please me to no end if you would use them to get away for a while to give this major decision some further deep consideration in one of Nature's quieter offices.

Bon voyage,

Dad

30 Life's
Report Card

My Dear Daughter:

You know that I have always maintained a board of directors made up of sound thinkers, fine leaders, and each one as independent as can be. That often leads to some pretty stormy sessions in our boardroom before six such strong-minded individuals settle a matter in full accord. While they are among the best in business, I must admit that the usual tenor of our meetings is not common to most boardrooms and, as chairman, I am frequently called upon to break a tie vote. You have probably heard me refer to our board as my "rebellion clan."

Nothing could have been further from the truth yesterday, however, when the selection of your company's new president came up. Usually, deciding on a president for one of our companies constitutes grounds for open warfare among the clan. Not so, this time.

Since your name was among the three submitted to the directors, I chose to absent myself from the room, reminding the rest as I left that their sole responsibility was to pick the best person for the job, with no worry or concern as to what my personal feelings might be in the matter. (Why I bothered to remind them, I don't know, since they haven't worried about my feelings regarding most topics for many years now.)

I expected that, true to form, there would be hours of deliberation and a lot of gnashing of teeth before they arrived at their decision, so it was with great surprise that I received their call to rejoin the meeting in twenty minutes. The interim Chairman then stated that they had reached a decision which, for once, was unanimous – in favour of *you*. They averred that, as excellent as the qualifications of the other two candidates were, yours outstripped them and that the choice had been one of the easiest they have ever had to make. *This* from my cantankerous rebellious group? It was music to my ears. I knew you had the wherewithal for the post or I would never have encouraged you to throw your hat into the ring as a contender. It is tough enough being the boss's daughter *with* the proper credentials for a job; I would not have wanted to see you tackle this one without them. Some will still say, however, that you got to be president only because of our familial ties. They would not, of course, if they knew our board of directors.

So, as the bearers of the good news, it was with great happiness that your mother and I set off for our visit with your family at the cottage. I doubt that I will ever forget the marvellous scene our announcement created: the kids hooting with joy, Mother crying her eyes out, you trying to retain your composure, and your husband bursting with pride. If I am not mistaken, there was even a tear or two in his eyes at that moment. Of course the mist in mine had only been caused by the weed sprayer you had probably used on the lawn that day.

I have not enjoyed a holiday more over the last few years than this recent week spent with you and the rest of our family. Even with all the boisterous fun of calling you "President" at every turn, the great outdoors still had its magic way of cooling out our minds and bodies better than any tranquilizer ever invented. One evening, as I sat back watching everyone enjoying a barbecue by the peaceful lake, I thought it was the most beautiful sight that I had ever seen. Most of us pause all too seldom to drink in these best of times.

When I asked myself what was pleasing me most about the scene in front of me – aside from the evident good health of all, of course – I realized it was knowing that each and every member of the family was vigorously pursuing a goal and maximizing his talents. And I noted the self-confidence each had attained, which is very high on my personal list of all the wonderful things I could wish for my family. You, especially, stand in a class all of your own in this category.

I had to smile to myself as I observed you organizing everything (and everybody) for Mom's surprise birthday dinner that week. Your administrative abilities were clearly in full gear, with a sensitivity and consideration for everyone involved in your plans. I liked your presidential style and, as the awareness dawned on me, it gave me a great feeling of confidence knowing that you had reached the stage where you were fully capable of handling any of life's twists or turns without my help. That does not mean that I will no longer offer a word or two of advice now and then – whether it is asked for or not – but my guess is that it will seldom be required. Your ever-positive contribution to every aspect of your life, your creative development and pursuit of goals, your integrity, your generosity toward people, your discerning quickness of action in business, your continued learning programs, and your quest for knowledge have earned you highest grades in life's report card. In Phillip Bailey's words, you are living proof that, "It matters not how long we live, but how."

Your work within your community and for charitable organizations is more proof of the same. And I don't think that I have ever told you how especially I have admired your loyalty and assistance over the years to your friends and colleagues who had fallen on hard times. You have consistently given to this world your time, your energy, and your talents, making it a better place to live in for a great many people.

As I turn the pages of my life story and get nearer to the end of this thrilling book that I am so enjoying, one particular observation of Horace's comes to mind: ''We rarely find anyone who can say he lived a happy life, and who, content with his life, can retire from the world like a satisfied guest.'' I am not ready to break up the party and go home yet, but when I do, it will be with the enormous satisfaction of having shared my life with the most wonderful daughter any father has ever had. I tell you this now for I believe that there have been a great many loving fathers who meant to tell their daughters the very same thing, but found it rather hard to communicate it from the grave! I want my acknowledgement to you to be on record long ahead of time.

I shall keep on popping by now and then to see how you are doing. The rest of the time I shall be tending the other areas of my ''garden'' – as usual planting a little more here, pruning a bit there, harvesting, and, most of all, enjoying the beautiful scenery. From among all the advice I have offered you over the years, there is none better that I could leave you with now than to remind you to stop often to enjoy the scenery and smell the many flowers of your own garden.

As to *my* report card? When the Maker gets around to grading that, I hope I will have earned my highest marks in child raising. If I do, it will be because you made it my favourite subject in life.

With much love,

Your Very Proud Dad